A letter from the Series Editors

Dear Teacher,

This series of teachers' resource books has developed from Pilgrims' involvement in running courses for learners of English and for teachers and teacher trainers.

Our aim is to pass on ideas, techniques and practical activities which we know work in the classroom. Our authors, both Pilgrims' teachers and like-minded colleagues in other organisations, present accounts of innovative procedures which will broaden the range of options available to teachers working within communicative and humanistic approaches.

We would be very interested to receive your impressions of the series. If you notice any omissions that we ought to record in future editions, or if you think of any interesting variations, please let us know. We will be glad to acknowledge all contributions that we are able to use.

Seth Lindstromberg
Series Editor

Mario Rinvolucri
Series Consultant

Pilgrims Language Courses
Canterbury
Kent
CT1 3HG
England

David Cranmer

David Cranmer was born in Leamington Spa in 1954. He studied at Cambridge and London universities to become a musicologist but subsequently chose a career in English Language Teaching. He has worked in Britain, Iran, Holland and, since 1981, in Lisbon, first as a teacher and teacher–trainer at the British Council (until 1993), and now as a lecturer at the Catholic University. He has published many articles on ELT, in journals such as *Practical English Teaching*, *Modern English Teacher*, *The Teacher Trainer* and *The Journal for Teachers of English in the Portuguese-speaking World* (formerly the *Portuguese Newsletter*), of which he is editor. He has contributed to *At the Chalkface* (Edward Arnold 1985) and *More Recipes for Tired Teachers* (Addison-Wesley 1991), and is co-author with Clement Laroy of *Musical Openings* in this series. Since settling in Lisbon he has resumed his activities as an organist and musicologist.

Dedication

To Teresa,
who, the first time I took her out, patiently listened to
me talking about little but the ideas in this book
. . . and married me.

Contents

Index of activities   vi

Introduction   1

Chapter 1 Establishing work patterns   5

Chapter 2 Noticing   32

Chapter 3 Imagination and creativity   61

Chapter 4 Thinking   90

Chapter 5 Feedback   115

Bibliography   123

'The fish in the water is silent, the animal on the earth is noisy, the
bird in the air is singing,
But man has in him the silence of the sea, the noise of the earth
and the music of the air.'
Rabindranath Tagore

Index of activities

Note: the Activities marked with an asterisk (*) should be done early in a course if possible.

	ACTIVITY	FOCUS
1 ESTABLISHING WORK PATTERNS	*1.1 Taking the plunge	The realities of being an advanced learner: raising student awareness of how they should be approaching their language studies
	*1.2 The class contract	Making expectations clear
	*1.3 The letter diary	Setting up a system of student–teacher communication
	*1.4 Symbol shadows	Understanding one another better
	*1.5 Magnet, island or bridge?	Awareness of role, especially in the class
	*1.6 The happiness cake	Feeling good together
	1.7 What went right? What went wrong?	Reflection on good and bad learning experiences
	1.8 Thought for the day	Sharing a beautiful thought or insight; Getting the lesson off to a good start
	1.9 Ups and downs	Awareness of the diversity of personal rhythms
	1.10 Concentration span	Awareness of diversity in concentration span
	1.11 Principles of memorising	Understanding how memory functions
	1.12 'The half is greater than the whole'	Applying the principles of memorising: memorising when to use *do* and *make*
2 NOTICING	2.1 So that's how you say it	Noticing language
	*2.2 Encouraging reading	Discussion on reading outside class
	2.3 A project on an English-speaking country	Raising student awareness about English as a *world* language
	2.4 Culture project	Encouraging identification with the target-language culture
	2.5 News project	Being awake to events in the world
	2.6 The classroom	Noticing objects that surround us day by day
	2.7 Parks and gardens	Noticing trees, flowers and people's behaviour
	2.8 A visit to the market	Vocabulary relating to markets; Shades of colour
	2.9 My way to work	Noticing things as we go about our daily business
	2.10 'Fine weather for ducks'	Noticing the weather and its effect on people
	2.11 'That's nice!'	Eradicating banal vocabulary

		ACTIVITY		FOCUS
3	**IMAGINATION**	3.1	The licence	Allowing ourselves to be bizarre
	AND CREATIVITY	3.2	Beauty and the Beast	Adding description to narrative; Encouraging imagination
		*3.3	If a table could speak . . .	Stimulating the imagination
		3.4	People in paintings	Imagining ourselves in someone else's shoes; Revision of question forms
		3.5	Painting into poem	Stimulating the imagination; Writing poetry
		3.6	Musical description	Visualising a scene through music
		3.7	Musical narrative	Visualising a story through music; Vocabulary relating to battles
		3.8	'Pigs might fly'	Ten principles of creativity
		3.9	Creative principles applied	Extending the use of the ten creative principles
4	**THINKING**	*4.1	Composition stages	Raising student awareness of the stages they should go through when they write a composition
		4.2	The brainstorm plan	Generating and organising ideas for a composition
		4.3	The mind map plan	Generating and organising ideas for a composition
		4.4	The mind map summary	Summary writing using mind map plans
		4.5	The random object	What to do when ideas won't come
		4.6	Lethargy and the lemon	Solving the problems that arise with a class
		4.7	Plus, minus and interesting	A framework for discussing and sharing insights into learning and teaching issues
		4.8	The PMI composition	Applying the plus, minus, interesting technique to composition writing
5	**FEEDBACK**	5.1	After correction I	Making sure learners benefit from correction; Encouraging checking and editing
		5.2	After correction II	Making sure learners benefit from correction; Encouraging checking and editing
		5.3	Counselling	Discussing progress with students
		5.4	Formal assessment	Leading students to be realistic about their final grade

Introduction

The purpose of this book

What is it that makes a successful language learner? In my experience, learners that are successful show a combination of some or all of a number of characteristics. They are intelligent (though not necessarily exceptional), conscientious and hardworking, they are committed to what they are doing and try to enter into the spirit of the language they are trying to learn, they are self-aware and self-critical, they are awake to the world by reading widely and knowing what is going on, they reflect on what they discover, have a coherent sense of what they think, are imaginative and get on well with their teacher and colleagues. In short, it is a series of human qualities that leads to successful language learning. This is true at any level but it is more than ever true of the learner that succeeds in going beyond an intermediate competence to become an advanced speaker/writer.

If this is so, then the traditional content of 'advanced level' courses, that is to say, courses that aim to take learners from an upper intermediate level to an advanced one, often fail to provide what is really needed. While they may include advanced grammar and vocabulary, topics or skills, and possibly literature, valuable and necessary though these certainly are, human skills as such find little place. The consequences of this are very apparent if you listen to the complaints of teachers at these levels discussing the difficulties they are trying to cope with. Here are some typical examples:

a 'My students keep missing classes and don't do their homework' (i.e. they lack the necessary commitment).

b 'My students speak and write like a literal translation of their own language' (i.e. they don't enter into the spirit of the target language).

c 'My students go on making the same basic mistakes' (i.e. they are not sufficiently self-critical).

d 'My students are unadventurous in structures and vocabulary' (i.e. they don't get sufficient contact with the language to be able to enrich these areas or fail to apply language once it has been met).

e 'My students don't seem to know much about anything, so it is impossible to teach the language to say it with' (i.e. they are not awake to the world and/or do not reflect on it).

f 'My students' compositions either miss the point or the points don't follow on from one to the next' (i.e. are not coherent and properly planned).

g 'My students write such dull compositions' (i.e. they lack imagination).

h 'My students rarely if ever speak' (i.e. they don't interact well with the teacher and colleagues).

With the exception chiefly of the last of these complaints, it is in writing that these problems are most apparent, which gives rise to the most common blanket complaint of all, 'They just can't write!'

This book aims to encourage the human skills that all learners have and to develop them further. Most of the activities, especially in Chapters 2 to 5, do so in relation to writing. Although all of the activities are particularly appropriate for use with upper intermediate and lower advanced students, genuinely advanced learners also derive benefit and a good deal of enjoyment from them. Where I have found that they can also be used fruitfully at a mid intermediate level, I have drawn attention to this in the introduction to the activity concerned.

What is in this book

The book is divided into five chapters.

● Chapter 1 is about establishing good learning habits and creating a positive working atmosphere.

● Chapter 2 is about going beyond the world we restrict ourselves to and noticing things. Some of the activities encourage students to read widely, to notice the language that arises and to apply what they find by doing projects. Others are concerned with practical observation tasks done outside the classroom. The aim of these activities is above all to provide material for compositions in the same way as novelists draw their material from observation of the real world.

● Chapter 3 is about imagination and creativity. It works on the premise, which no student of mine has ever yet succeeded in disproving, that everyone has an imagination and an ability to create. Although some people genuinely do feel blocked in this area, with practice anyone can learn to use and enjoy using their imagination and creativity. The activities here develop both of these by applying ideas from the visual arts and music to creative writing.

● Chapter 4 is about thinking. We all know how to think, but that doesn't mean that there aren't ways of improving our thinking. This chapter looks at the thinking stages involved in composition writing, ways of planning compositions and frameworks for discussing problems affecting learning in the class. It also offers a way of tackling the vexed area of summary writing.

● Chapter 5 suggests various types of feedback: an approach to the correction and follow-up of written work, which has an important role in underpinning the writing tasks in the book, counselling students about their difficulties and providing a way of enabling students to be involved in the giving of formal assessments at the end of a course, if you need to give them.

How to use this book

This is not a coursebook, nor an outline for an advanced level course. It is a resource book of activities to be used alongside any other resources you have available. In my own teaching these activities have become the backbone of my long-term planning at higher levels.

In a course of three to five hours per week, you will need to spread the material in this book over about two years. It is important to do some of these activities early in a course, in order to establish ground rules and good learning habits (they are marked with an asterisk (*) in the Index of Activities on pages vi–vii). On the other hand, since many of the activities described here will be very new to your students, you have to allow time for them to assimilate them.

The activities I describe in this book all follow the same format. In the margin you will find the 'focus' of the activity, that is to say what it aims to achieve, the materials you might need and the timing (which can be very variable). Many of the activities have an introductory paragraph, explaining further points about the rationale or anything else I think you need to be aware of. If any preparation is needed, I have described it next. The procedure is divided into a series of steps giving clear instructions as to what to do. In some cases there are notes at the end of the activity. These generally give an idea of the kind of reactions to expect from your students, or points that have arisen when I have used the activity.

I find I like to take part in the activities myself. When my students do a practical exercise out of class, I do it too. When they do a project, so do I. It's the only way I can be in tune with them and what they are doing. Otherwise I forget from year to year exactly what it feels like to do the activities. In some cases I have specifically suggested you do the activity too but, if you can find the time or energy, it is always a good idea to do so. Doing these activities again and again reminds me of the challenge they represent and my students seem to feel better, watching me tackle the same tasks as themselves. Like my students, I sometimes run into difficulties, which reminds me of my own fallibility, which in turn reminds me to be realistic about what I expect from them. I often do the same writing task as my students, in Portuguese (in which I am as advanced as they are in English), and get one of them to correct it. This is an especially useful and humbling experience – useful to them as an 'editing' task, giving them insights into learner error-making, as well as to me in providing feedback; humbling to me as I find myself making errors comparable to theirs. This whole exercise is thoroughly beneficial to the solidarity between my students and myself.

To conclude

This book has come into existence above all for three reasons. Firstly, my own students have gained enormously from these activities and I would like others to benefit too. Secondly, many of my colleagues over the past ten years have encouraged me to write it. But most important of all, this book is a statement of faith – that in the end there are only so many structures, for example, in a language and only so many ways of teaching them, but the people we teach are infinite in their variety. This is a book about working with people, and there is nothing so rewarding as watching people grapple with themselves and the world . . . and growing through the experience.

Lisbon, March 1995

CHAPTER 1

Establishing work patterns

'The teacher who walks in the shadow of the temple, among his followers, gives not of his wisdom but rather of his faith and his lovingness.

If he is indeed wise he does not bid you enter the house of his wisdom, but rather leads you to the threshold of your own mind.'
Kahlil Gibran

This chapter provides a general framework for language learning at more advanced levels. It looks at learner and teacher expectations, establishing a positive working environment and raising awareness of how people function. These are fundamentals in any learning situation but particularly critical for more advanced learners.

TAKING THE PLUNGE

Learners rarely stop to reflect on how they should be going about their learning – what they need to invest and how. It is important that they do so at all levels, but at more advanced levels it is absolutely critical since they have to get used to doing more and more on their own, to taking the responsibility for their own learning. Do this task in the first or second lesson of a course.

Preparation

Make a class set of the Handout on pages 7–8.

Procedure

1 Ask your class what they think are the main problems of being a more advanced learner. They usually talk about difficult vocabulary, complex structures and other language items. Accept these points but put it to them that there is often a much more fundamental problem, namely how they go about their learning. If any student raises any of the more fundamental areas outlined in the handout, use this as a direct springboard into the next step.
2 Give each student a copy of the Handout on pages 7–8. Ask them to read the text and answer the questions. Set a time limit of thirty minutes. Tell your students that you will want to collect the

1.1

FOCUS
The realities of being an advanced learner: raising student awareness of how they should be approaching their language studies

MATERIALS
A class set of the Handout 'Being a good learner'

TIME
40–60 minutes, plus 10–20 minutes in a follow-up lesson

completed handouts in to read, but that you are interested in what they say, not in how correct the English is. (They may need longer to answer the last question properly, so be flexible if you see that this is the case with your students.) With students that finish early, take the opportunity to speak to individuals and discuss some of their answers.

3 When they have finished, initiate a discussion about what they have read and written. Ask them if they feel they have learnt anything important that they perhaps hadn't thought about before. Encourage an exchange of views among the members of the class. Collect in the completed handouts.

4 Later, go through the handouts, noting down any points you want to use for feedback and any you want to keep for your own reference. Make comments on the handouts about the contents where you feel this would be helpful to the student but don't correct. In a follow-up lesson, preferably the lesson immediately following, go over any points that emerged from the handouts. In particular, you may want to draw attention to reference materials you would recommend. (The *Longman Dictionary of English Language and Culture* is an invaluable source and provides grammatical information as well as encyclopedia-type entries for important cultural items.) Return the handouts to your students.

VARIATION

In Step 3, after the students have completed their handouts, put them into groups of four to compare and discuss what they wrote. In particular, ask them to discuss the specific contexts where the quantum leap would be important and the sort of tasks that might involve the three areas of observing, imagining and thinking. This can be very valuable but you will need to set aside about twenty minutes extra.

NOTE

I have included this rather 'dry' activity at the specific request of colleagues at the British Council, Lisbon. They have been using an earlier version of the handout for some years and have grown to consider it indispensable at the beginning of an advanced course. I owe the variation to my colleague David Hardisty.

HANDOUT FOR ACTIVITY 1.1

Being a good advanced learner

Many learners of English manage to reach a level where they can understand, speak and write for everyday purposes. Yet only a relatively small proportion of these people ever become genuinely advanced users of the language, though many make the attempt. As you are just beginning a course in more advanced English, it is important for you to be aware of what you need to do and how to go about it, so that you can make a success of your course.

You are going to read a short text, with a series of tasks to do as you read. This will provide an opportunity to reflect on your learning and, through your answers to the tasks, will give your teacher valuable information about you as a learner, so that he or she can give you greater guidance for the future.

Beyond spoon-feeding

In many language courses the teaching at lower levels tends to follow a pattern of what could be described as 'spoon-feeding' – the teacher chooses the elements of the language to teach (the food), plans how to present it (puts it onto a spoon) and teaches (feeds) the learners with it, as if they were children. However, just as children become progressively more independent and in due course have to assume full responsibility for themselves as adults, so learners of a language, as they advance, have to become more independent and assume greater responsibility for their own learning.

To be successful at an advanced level, you will have to commit yourself not only to attending classes but also to spending a substantial amount of time studying out of class. This should partly be directed by your teacher (homework and preparation) and partly through your own initiative.

A typical student with three to five hours of English classes per week should expect to spend about the same number of hours studying out of class – doing grammar exercises and writing tasks, learning vocabulary, reading extensively, and so on. The fewer hours you have with a teacher, the more you will have to work on your own. Without this kind of commitment you cannot expect to make a lot of progress.

1 How many hours of English classes do you have each week? ....
2 How many more hours can you commit to learning English each week? ....

It is easy to commit yourself to a theoretical number of hours per week, but unless you set aside particular days and times, you will keep finding you are too busy doing other things. So decide now which days and times you are going to dedicate to studying English. ....

3 In the light of your commitment, how much progress do you expect to make? In what areas (e.g. listening/speaking/reading/writing, accuracy/ fluency)? Be specific about your objectives.

....
....

Ways of studying

Making good progress depends not only on how much time you spend but also how you go about studying. For example, how do you organise the things you want to learn?

4 Write about how you organise the notes you take in class and the things you want to learn when studying on your own.

....

5 What techniques do you use to memorise things?

....

6 When you are studying alone, you need good reference materials. What dictionaries, grammar books and other materials do you have?

....

The quantum leap

Ironically, one of the greatest problems that often arises among more advanced learners is the fact that they can already function in English for a lot of everyday purposes and, instead of extending their knowledge, go on just using what they already know. To be successful at an advanced level, this is not enough. You have to make a 'quantum leap', in other words a significant jump towards something much more sophisticated and wide-ranging. You have to aim to function like a mature, well-educated native speaker of the language. This means that you need to be able to draw upon your experience of the world and to have a reasonable, though not specialist, knowledge of any subject you are speaking or writing about. The content is vitally important, because if this is too limited, your language will be correspondingly limited – you won't need and therefore won't use more advanced structures and vocabulary.

7 How old are you? ....
8 What areas do you feel you have some knowledge about?

....

9 In what areas do you feel you have very little knowledge?

....

There are three areas that contribute substantially to making the quantum leap and particularly to writing in a more sophisticated way: observation, imagination and thinking.

10 Do you consider yourself to be good at
   a observing? ....
   b imagining? ....
   c thinking? ....
   Explain your answers.

....

Good luck with your advanced course!

THE CLASS CONTRACT

Your students have expectations of you and you have expectations of your students. It is important for everyone to be clear what these are. One way of achieving this is to draw up a contract between you and your class. I make this the main activity of my first lesson with any new group.

FOCUS
Making expectations clear

MATERIALS
A blank sheet of paper

TIME
45 minutes

Procedure

1 Divide the class into pairs. Ask each pair to draw up two lists: what they expect of you and what they think you should expect of them. Give them about fifteen minutes for this. Meanwhile you make a list of what you expect of them and what you think they should expect of you.

2 Tell your students that you want to draw up a contract with them based on the expectations that they and you have just noted down. Divide the board into two columns: '(your name) agrees to' and 'The class agrees to'. Appoint a class secretary to make a fair copy of what you are about to write on the board and give them a sheet of paper to write it on. Nobody else need write anything. Negotiate with the class, on the basis of what you and they wrote down, what they can expect of you and you are willing to abide by, and vice versa. Draw up an agreed wording on the board for the secretary to copy. When it is complete, you and all your students must sign the secretary's fair copy.

3 Take the fair copy of the contract. Make enough copies to give one to each student. Distribute the copies next lesson and stick the original on the classroom wall. If any new students join the class, invite them to read the contract and sign it. Give them a copy too.

4 At regular intervals, e.g. once a week in a one-month course, or beginning, mid and end of terms in a one-year course, hold a brief discussion with the class on how well everyone is abiding by the contract. If you're all doing well, give yourselves a round of applause. If not, discuss what is going wrong and what you might do about it. This might include discussion as to whether you are slipping or the demands of the contract are unrealistic.

NOTE
Drawing up the contract provides you with an important opportunity to discuss expectations about homework. I give out a list of rules, e.g. telling them how long I give them to do their homework in, and to write compositions on alternate lines so that I have room to indicate the corrections. So far every class has agreed to abide by them. Here is an example of the contract I drew up with one group:

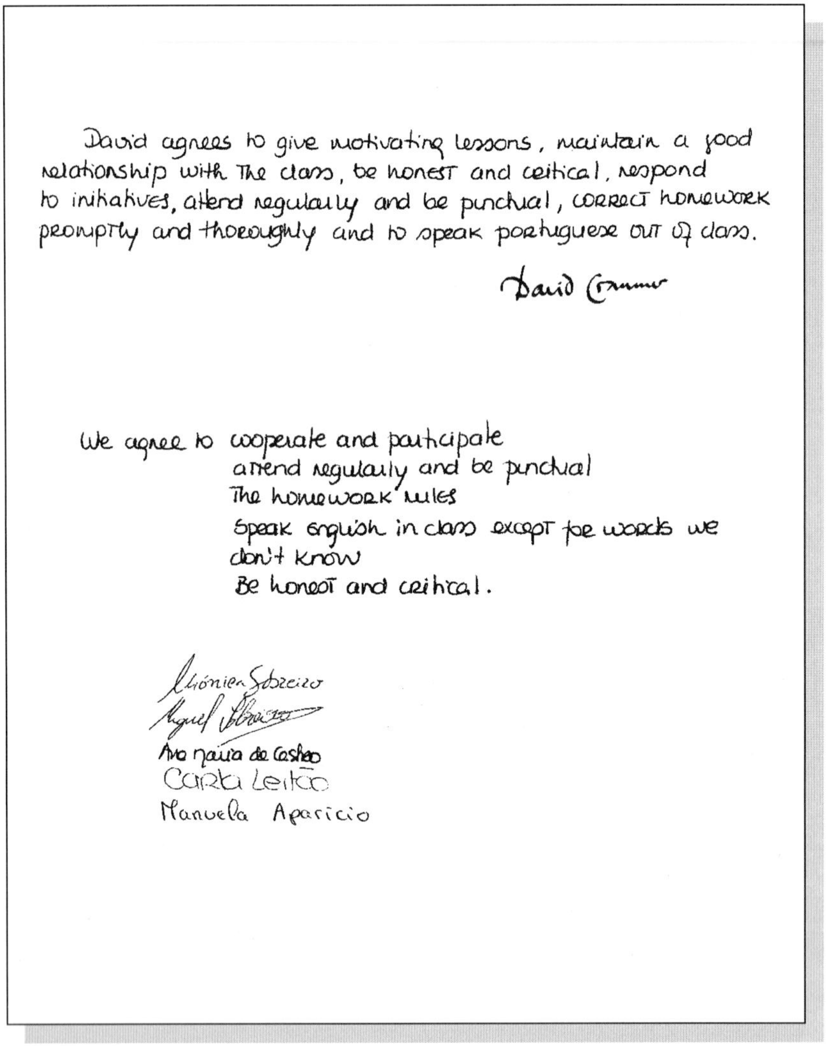

David agrees to give motivating lessons, maintain a good relationship with the class, be honest and critical, respond to initiatives, attend regularly and be punctual, correct homework promptly and thoroughly and to speak portuguese out of class.

David Cromm

We agree to cooperate and participate
attend regularly and be punctual
The homework rules
Speak english in class except for words we don't know
Be honest and critical.

Mónica Sobreiro
Miguel Ferreira
Ana Maria de Castro
Carla Leitão
Manuela Aparicio

Fig. 1

ACKNOWLEDGEMENT
I first heard of the concept of class contracts from Cynthia Beresford. Puchta and Schratz (1993), pp. 57–65, give a carefully elaborated procedure for drawing up contracts with teenage classes.

THE LETTER DIARY

Some teachers like their students to maintain a 'learner diary', reflecting on how their learning is going and possibly writing about other things from their lives outside English lessons. Others like to write their students a letter introducing themselves as a starting point for a regular exchange of letters between students and teacher. This activity sets up a system of student–teacher communication that combines both ideas. I have used it with students whose English was barely lower intermediate, but it has been most successful with students of at least mid to upper intermediate level.

Preparation

Write a letter introducing yourself. The tone you set in your letter is important as it establishes an initial model for future exchanges. I like to write it the evening before I intend to hand it out, and to tell my students how I'm feeling and what I'm thinking about as well as to give plain autobiographical information. This encourages answers that similarly tell you how your students are feeling and what things are on their minds, not just a bare catalogue of where they live and how many brothers and sisters they have. At the end of the letter I mention briefly how I want them to go about answering my letter, which I explain in more detail in the lesson (see Step 2 below). Make photocopies of your letter, one for each student.

Procedure

1 Ask your students if they like receiving letters. As soon as someone says yes, tell them you've got a letter for them and give them a copy of your letter. Very quickly everyone else will want one, so hand out the rest of the letters and give the class a little while to read it. (If you have written a genuinely affectionate letter, you will see smiles and glowing faces as they read.)

2 Tell your students you would like them to get a notebook and stick your letter on the first page. Invite them to answer your letter as if it were the first entry in a diary. Tell them you would like them to write as regularly as possible in their 'diary' and to give it to you whenever they have written something. You will comment on their entry, briefly or at greater length, as you find appropriate, and may add points you want to tell the student concerned, for example, any worries you have about the student's work. Stress that the purpose of the diary is to provide a channel of communication between your students and yourself (and that this will remain totally private), and to provide free writing practice – you will not be correcting it but responding to it as you would any letter you receive.

1.3

FOCUS
Setting up a system of student–teacher communication

MATERIALS
A class set of a letter introducing yourself

TIME
5 minutes

NOTES

a I make the letter diary strictly voluntary, something that won't be graded, that can be done as often or as rarely as my students wish. At the same time I emphasise the advantages of taking up the invitation to write – the extra writing practice it gives them, the help it gives me in understanding them as people (their circumstances, the difficulties and successes they may be going through that affect their learning). I sometimes recount particular instances of former students of mine that have benefited particularly from writing, more or less regularly.

b The issue of correction is important. Some students ask me to correct their diary but I am strict in insisting that I will respond just as I would to a letter in real life – I don't send back the letter I received covered in red ink, I just answer the letter. At the same time, if there is a serious error I think they should be aware of, I tell them in the answer, but in normal letter-style, not teacher-correction-style. I only break the rule of not correcting if specifically requested by a student who is about to do a public examination and I feel that the correction will provide real feedback to help the student pass.

c You need to be ready for an initial burst of enthusiasm and set aside some time to answer the first diary entries, since they tend to come back all at once. In my experience, however, only a small number maintain a diary with any regularity, mainly students that really are keen on the idea, and the correspondence with them can be very rewarding.

1.4

FOCUS
Understanding
one another
better

MATERIALS
A blank sheet of
paper

TIME
20–30 minutes

SYMBOL SHADOWS

'What you are you do not see, what you see is your shadow.'
Rabrindinath Tagore

This is a good activity for the second or third lesson of a course.

Procedure

1 Write the above quotation on the board. Discuss it briefly with your students. Then draw a symbolic representation of your own 'shadow' on the board – various symbols that in some way represent you and things/people that are important to you. I usually draw a circle or cloud first, to serve as an outline, and put the symbols inside. There are no prizes for brilliant drawing! When you have drawn your shadow explain the symbols to your students.

2 Ask them to draw their own shadows. When they have done that, if you have a small class, ask them one by one to explain their shadow to everyone else. If your class has more than around a dozen students, divide the class into groups of between six and a dozen to do the same. If you remain in whole-class formation, make sure the explanations are directed towards everyone in the class, not just you. If you have groups, monitor them discreetly, again making sure the explanations are directed towards their colleagues rather than you.

3 As a follow-up task, either in class or for homework, ask your students to write up the explanation of their symbols. I like to display these around the classroom so that the students can read about their colleagues.

Here are two example shadows done by students with their own uncorrected explanations of the symbols:

Fig. 2

It's a sort of box because I'm very closed in myself, and with a locker because I don't let everybody in. In it there's a book, a radio/tape recorder and a TV, it's mainly what I spend my days doing when I'm not at school or studying. There are also faces of boys and girls: these are my friends, and they're in a little box apart because I don't reveal myself to them, I don't have as many close friends as Id like to.

Beatriz

Fig. 3

I think the most important characteristic of my life is that I am always in a rush and my thoughts are divided in very different things – I study History at the University, which I like very much, but as it is difficult to get a job with an History degree, I also study English and French. Meanwhile I never refuse the opportunity to earn some money in part-time jobs, because I don't like to be always asking money to my parents and besides I am always arguing with my father. I also make big efforts to save money in my lunches.

I find I have got the fortune of having several good friends and I like very much to be with them some time but this is not possible, and some of them don't understand why I can not share their happy hours on their little problems. I get very sad with this.

I like very much to be alone at home, watching TV, reading, . . . – I am always dreaming of having a place of my own.

I make many questions and I hesitate a lot as to the choices I need to do and my sentimental life is, perhaps the best example of this fact.

I am looking forward for the day when I will have more time for my friends and to do more often some other things I like – to go to the cinema, to swim, to learn more about other subject I like, as music and painting, for exemple, etc. . . .

Ana Sofia

NOTE

With students that have a positive attitude this activity is a favourite. Occasionally (extremely rarely with students over twenty years old), you may be working with individuals who react more negatively, e.g. by refusing to take part. Don't insist – they have a right to refuse to take part. They may well change their minds once they see their colleagues doing and enjoying the task. Otherwise, once the rest of the class is busily working, ask them discreetly what their difficulty is. Discussing the problem normally defuses it and leads to a positive reaction to future activities that may be rather different from what they are used to. You will, in any case, at this early stage in the course, get a very clear idea of the individuals you are dealing with and their attitudes to what you are trying to do.

MAGNET, ISLAND OR BRIDGE?

The way students relate to one another is extremely important in creating a conducive working environment. If, for example, there is fierce competition or a tendency to laugh at others' mistakes, the atmosphere in class will be threatening, the students will become defensive and their learning will suffer.

Do this activity early in a course to raise the issue and encourage helpful attitudes. Make reference to it again later if you feel that there are problems in this area that need airing.

Procedure

1 If you have a magnet, show it to the class and check they know what it is called. Otherwise, you may need to explain it in the next step. On the board draw three columns, heading them respectively 'magnet', 'island' and 'bridge'. Divide your class into pairs and ask them to draw up a list of characteristics of each. Allow no more than five minutes for this. Ask the pairs what they came up with and write the characteristics in the columns on the board.

2 Ask your students to think for a moment about the way they act in various social contexts, e.g. at parties, with colleagues, in the family – more like a magnet, an island or a bridge? Most of us are a mixture and different circumstances bring out predominantly one or more aspect. Divide the class into groups of five or six to discuss this briefly (five to ten minutes).

3 Ask them, still in groups, to discuss which attitude – the magnet, the island or the bridge – is most conducive to a good working environment in class and what that implies in terms of actual behaviour.

4 Discuss as a class the findings of the groups. They should, in general, feel that being a bridge is the most conducive and that it implies a spirit of co-operation, participating, helping others, including others. At the same time, a magnet may, on occasions, act as a catalyst to encourage shyer members of a class. Discuss with the class when/how a magnet might be a positive element in a class and when/how a negative one.

5 Extend the discussion to how bridges can be formed out of class. Draw up a list on the board. Here are some ideas that students of mine have suggested:

- having coffee with colleagues before/after lessons
- going to class or going home with a colleague
- exchanging phone numbers (to chat, to discuss homework, to find out what went on in class if they were absent)
- meeting socially with one or more colleagues (e.g. going to the cinema, theatre, a concert, on a picnic, visiting somewhere)

6 Give your students a few minutes to discuss with those sitting near them which of these ideas they feel are most appropriate to

1.5

FOCUS
Awareness of role, especially in the class

MATERIALS
A magnet (optional)

TIME
30 minutes

them and how they intend to implement them. It is better in this phase to let pairs/groups form spontaneously than to impose them. Ask a few members of the class what conclusions they came to.

NOTES

a It is important for students to work predominantly in groups in this activity. In whole-class formation many students find Steps 2 and 3 rather threatening.

b In Step 2 the answers students give are not to be taken at face value. One who says 'I don't know' is acting as an island, while one who says 'I tend to be a bit of an island', by sharing that, is acting as a bridge, and someone who brags about being a bridge, by attracting attention is actually a magnet. You need to decide, according to your teaching context and your sense of the individuals involved, whether or not to draw your students' attention to the real implications of what they are saying.

c This activity can be helpful if you are having trouble with the dynamics of the group (too many islands and/or magnets). I like to use it at key points in a course, e.g. the beginning/end of terms in a year-long course, when several new students have joined an already existing class or are about to leave to join another class.

d Some students may want to isolate themselves. Encourage them gently to be sociable but it is ultimately their decision.

ACKNOWLEDGEMENT
This activity is a descendant of one called 'Talheres' (Cutlery) in *Relações Humanas Interpessoais* (Fritzen 1987).

1.6

FOCUS
Feeling good
together

MATERIALS
None

TIME
20–30 minutes

THE HAPPINESS CAKE

Do this activity either early in the course to help your class to 'gel', or as a preliminary to Activity 4.3 *The mind map plan*. It demands a certain maturity of approach, so it may be better not to do it with potentially 'giggly' classes.

Procedure

1 Ask everyone to think for a moment about the ingredients for happiness. Tell everyone to imagine they are going to bake a happiness cake. What ingredients and what spices would they put in? Ask them to work alone and write down the ingredients and spices for their cake. Allow five minutes for this. You do it too.

2 If you have a small class (up to about twelve), ask each member in turn to tell the others (not just you) about the ingredients and spices for their cake. You tell them your list last. If you have a larger class, divide it into groups of six to a dozen, and get them

to do the same. Monitor the groups and when they have finished, ask them to report back to the whole class. Again tell them your ingredients and spices last.

NOTE

People's lists have much in common but can also differ noticeably. Also, what for some are main ingredients, for others are spices (e.g. money). For this reason, unless it happens spontaneously, it is best not to try to come to a consensus or build up a class list, but to respect individual needs and priorities. Here, however, is a consensus list that the students in one of my classes came up with:

Main ingredients	*Spices*
health	money
dreaming	music
study and work	mixture of responsibility and
family and friends	irresponsibility
love	time
freedom	tolerance
commitment	contentment
objectives and the will to	difficulties
achieve them	tears
honesty	humour
smiles	madness
understanding	good food and drink
feeling unafraid	
being ourselves, not as others would	
wish us	
feeling wanted and respected	
sharing	
fulfilment	

ACKNOWLEDGEMENT

This activity is derived from an idea I read in *Relações Humanas Interpessoais* (Fritzen 1987).

1.7

FOCUS
Reflection on
good and bad
learning
experiences

MATERIALS
None

TIME
20 minutes

WHAT WENT RIGHT? WHAT WENT WRONG?

Whenever I've been a student, I've always worked hardest and learnt most with teachers I liked and respected. This activity aims to draw attention to how crucial the teacher-student relationship is to learning.

Procedure

1 Talk to your students about your own good and bad learning experiences and the extent to which these correlated with good and bad relationships with your teachers.

2 Tell your students to draw two columns. In the first they are to list teachers they remember getting on well with and in the other those they got on badly with. Divide the class into groups of four or five and ask them to tell one another about these teachers and the effect they had on their learning.

3 Bring the students back together as a whole class and ask them what they feel are the main things that contribute to a good relationship between students and their teacher. In my experience the most important thing is regular, honest communication, because everything else both depends on this and can be remedied through this. Your students may come up with other points but be sure to emphasise the importance of regular, honest communication.

EXTENSION

As a follow up, either in class (allow 30 to 40 minutes for this) or for homework, get your students to write about their positive and negative learning experiences.

NOTE

This task may be embarrassing if you are teaching a group that has been at your institution for some time, learning from various of your colleagues. Tell your students only to refer to *good* learning experiences with your colleagues, but both good and bad experiences at other institutions. Explain that this is to avoid them or you feeling embarrassed.

THOUGHT FOR THE DAY

Procedure

1 At the beginning of each lesson write at the top of the board a quotation or thought that you think is worth sharing. Leave it there throughout the lesson.
2 If one or more of the class wants to discuss the 'thought', then let them. Otherwise just leave it on the board for reflection.

Here are some examples of thoughts for the day that I have used. They are all taken from *Stray Birds* (Tagore 1917), as are the various other quotations by him scattered through this book.

'If you shed tears when you miss the sun, you also miss the stars.'
'We read the world wrong and say that it deceives us.'
'The dry river-bed finds no thanks for its past.'
'If you shut your door to all errors, truth will be shut out.'
'The bird wishes it were a cloud. The cloud wishes it were a bird.'
'Wrong cannot afford defeat but Right can.'

Oriental proverbs are also a good source of thoughts for the day.

EXTENSIONS

1 Get the students to provide the quotations. One way of doing this is early on in the course ask each student to find two good quotations – beautiful or insightful thoughts – and bring them to class. These can act as a pool to draw from. When you are nearing the end of the supply, ask them each to bring two more. (Note: the quotations may be originally in English or translations from the student's own language or from some other language – you may need to provide some help with translations.)
2 At the end of the month/term/course, copy all the thoughts for the day onto one sheet. Distribute a copy to everyone in the class. Ask everyone to choose two or three they especially liked. Divide the class into groups of between four and six. Ask each group to discuss which thoughts they chose and why. Allow up to twenty minutes for this, monitoring what each group says. Bring the class together again. Chair a discussion about which thoughts came up in the various groups and the points raised around them. You may want to draw attention to points you heard as you were monitoring the groups. This whole activity may take anything up to an hour. I have also used this extension in the first lesson of a second term, to provide continuity from the previous terms and to involve new students in something we have already met before in class.

NOTE

My students are so accustomed to having a thought for the day that they complain if I forget.

1.8

FOCUS
Sharing a beautiful thought or insight; Getting the lesson off to a good start

MATERIALS
A quotation/ thought

TIME
Usually 2 minutes, sometimes 10

ACKNOWLEDGEMENTS

Margaret Pearson suggested to me the idea of students choosing the thought for the day. A student of mine, Filomena Afonso, suggested how this might be done. Extension 2 is based on an idea I read in *Relações Humanas Interpessoais* (Fritzen 1987).

1.9 UPS AND DOWNS

FOCUS
Awareness of the diversity of personal rhythms

MATERIALS
None

TIME
20–50 minutes

People function in very diverse ways and feel good/bad at very different times of day, week and year. Discovering this often comes as something of a revelation in class.

Procedure

1 Initiate a discussion on 'ups and downs' – when we feel better or not so good. Draw the first of these graphs on the board, showing your own ups and downs:

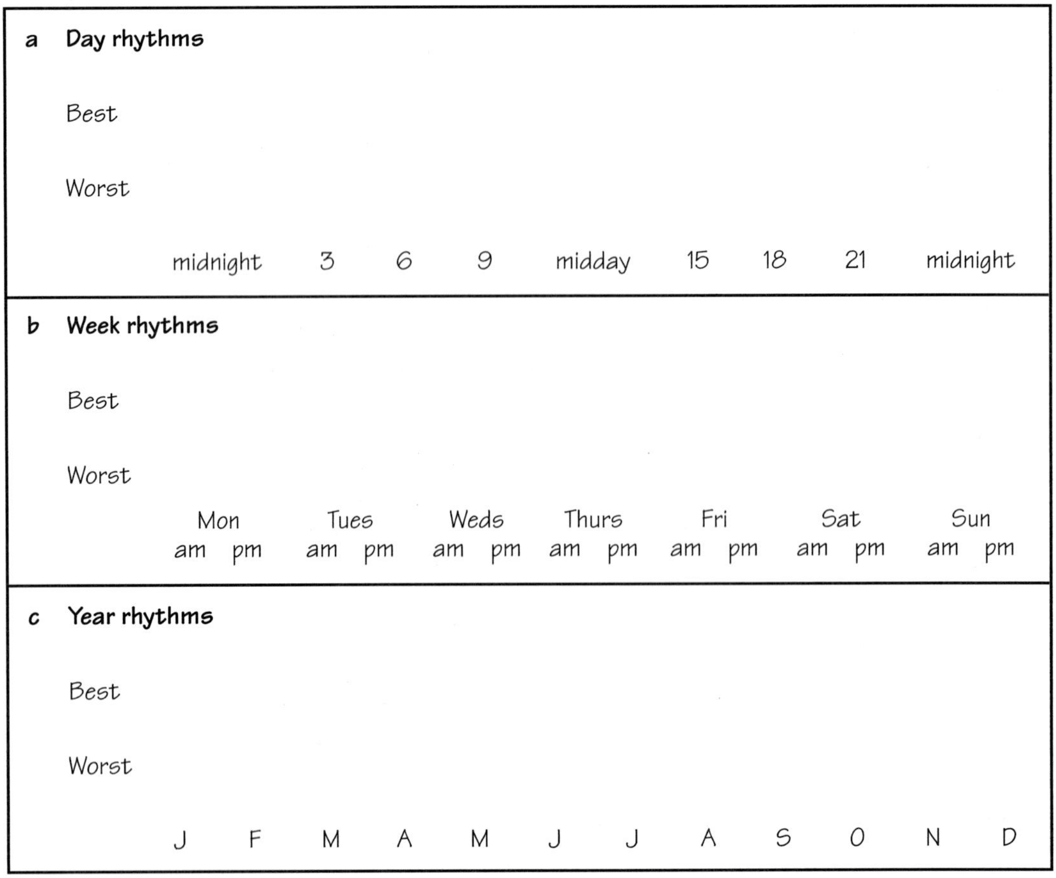

---

a   Day rhythms

Best

Worst

midnight   3   6   9   midday   15   18   21   midnight

---

b   Week rhythms

Best

Worst

	Mon	Tues	Weds	Thurs	Fri	Sat	Sun
	am pm	am pm	am pm	am pm	am pm	am pm	am pm

---

c   Year rhythms

Best

Worst

J   F   M   A   M   J   J   A   S   O   N   D

Fig. 4

Explain your day rhythms with reference to the graph. Mine for example looks like this:

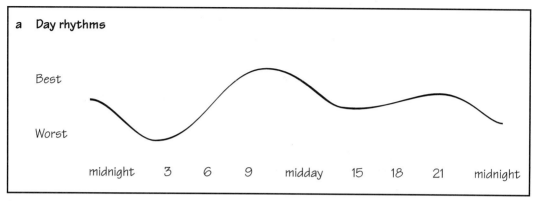

Fig. 5

From this you can see that I feel I'm at my best at about 10 a.m., that I'm not good in the afternoon but have a sustained good period in the evening, which starts to go down rapidly as midnight approaches.

Ask your students to copy the graph frame and complete it with their own day rhythms. When they are ready, ask them to explain their graph to their colleagues. If your class has more than about twelve students, divide the class into groups of up to twelve for this phase; monitor them and when they have finished get the groups to report to the whole class the kinds of things they found. Talking to my students I find that nearly everyone is down after lunch, but that some people are at their best in the morning, some in the late afternoon/evening, some at night.

2 Repeat this procedure for the weekly and yearly rhythms together, this time with you doing your graphs at the same time as your students. Again the patterns are very varied – not everyone hates Monday morning, some people prefer summer, others winter, and so on. It is important to be aware of when we feel best/worst irrespective of whether we are working or on holiday. We are trying to identify and compare our personal rhythms, not whether we like work!

NOTES

a Monthly rhythms don't tend to generate discussion – calendar months are rather arbitrary divisions and students generally clam up about women's monthly cycles. Most students are too young to be able to notice life rhythms but if you have a class of mature students, there may be some mileage to be got from talking about this area.

b A related activity 'Sharing learning rhythms' can be found in *The Confidence Book* (Davis & Rinvolucri 1990), pp. 59–60. This looks at personal rhythms during a course.

1.10

FOCUS
Awareness of
diversity in
concentration
span

MATERIALS
OHP and
transparency
(optional)

TIME
20–40 minutes

CONCENTRATION SPAN

Preparation

Copy the questions in Step 1 onto an OHP transparency. If you don't
have an OHP, just ask the questions as you go along.

Procedure

1 Initiate a discussion on concentration. Do your students find it
easy to concentrate? For long periods? Project the questions
below on an OHP and give the class about five minutes to
consider them.

   a In general are you good at concentrating or do you tend to drift off and
daydream?

   b Are there certain activities where you find your concentration is better?

   c Are you better at working in a series of short spurts or do you find it better to work in more sustained periods?

   d If you could divide the day as you wanted into periods of work, breaks
(including meals), spells of relaxation, how would you do so? In particular,
what do you consider the ideal length of working periods?

   e How compatible are your conclusions in the questions above with the
length of classes you have and the way they are divided into activities?

2 Discuss the questions with your students, also telling them how
you function in this respect. If you have a class of more than
about twelve, divide them into groups of up to twelve for this
step. Monitor them and, when they have finished, ask each group
to report their findings to the rest of the class.

3 In the light of the findings in Step 2, discuss how compatible these
are with the timetable restrictions within which you have to operate. Discuss whether any modifications might be possible in the
timetabling of your course to accommodate any generally per-
ceived incompatibility with students' rhythms. (See also Activity
1.9 *Ups and downs*.)

PRINCIPLES OF MEMORISING

Procedure

1 Write these questions on the board:

   a When you meet someone for the first time, do you find it easier to remember their name or their face?

   b If you have to memorise words, e.g. a poem, a part in a play or facts for an exam, do they stick easily or is memorising a painful process?

   c In class, if a teacher is explaining something new, is it sufficient for you for the teacher to explain it or do you feel a strong need to see it written down?

Discuss these questions with the class. Although it is difficult to draw conclusions from them, they raise the fundamental issue that language learning is intrinsically concerned with words. This creates a problem since many people experience difficulties of one kind or another when trying to remember words, as opposed to images.

2 Divide the class into pairs. Tell them that they are going to read a text about memorisation. Ask them to read it right through and then, to show that they have understood, to fill in the diagram that goes with it. Distribute the copies of both text and diagram on pages 24–5 and 26.

3 Monitor the class discreetly as they fill in their diagrams. Check that for item e) they don't draw a table with four legs! When your students are ready, go through the diagram with them. (The answers are: a) Recall, b) between 5 and 9 / 7±2, c) groups, d) visual, e) [check the tables they have drawn], f) orange, g) 24 hours, h) one week, i) form, j) add.) Tell them that they will soon be applying these principles to when to use *do* and when to use *make*.

VARIATION

Instead of making photocopies of the text and diagram, at the beginning of Step 2 copy the diagram onto the board for your students to recopy. Then give a talk on the principles of memorising, using the text as your brief and the diagram on the board as an *aide mémoire*. Tell them to complete their diagram as you give your talk. This variation, though more time-consuming, tends to be more effective: the 'dull' task of copying already sets the 'processing' in motion – draw attention to this – and the talk format makes the students concentrate hard.

FURTHER READING
Tony Buzan 1974, rev. 1982, 1989 *Use Your Head* BBC Publications

1.11

FOCUS
Understanding how memory functions

MATERIALS
Photocopies of the Handout 'Principles of memorising' and the Worksheet diagram for Step 2

TIME
40 minutes

HANDOUT FOR ACTIVITY 1.11

Principles of memorising

The concept of load

The capacity of the brain is enormous but it is not infinite. In trying to memorise we must try to make most efficient use of this capacity without overloading.

Research shows that learning occurs when we form patterns or manage to link new information to old. When it comes to working on new material the brain is most efficient when dealing with between five and nine (7±2) items or groups of items. Less than five is underworking it, more than nine results in overloading. Thus to try and memorise, for example, forty random vocabulary items would be completely unrealistic, but if they could be divided up into about seven groups, each of about six items, that is to say between five and nine 'patterns' of between five and nine items, this would be perfectly manageable.

Processing

It is often said that the best way to learn something is to have to teach it to someone else. The point that lies behind this is that to teach something effectively you have to have a clear knowledge of what it is you want to teach. In order to have this clear knowledge there has to be a process of assimilation – we have to absorb the information or habit. Occasionally this process of assimilation happens by itself but more often we need to resort to frequent repetition or some other form of conscious processing.

For many people, a strong visual element is helpful in the learning process – images reinforce words. It is useful therefore to add a visual element to words that need to be learnt. One way of doing this is to process the words into some visual form, e.g. a table (matrix), Venn diagram, mind map or flow chart. (You will see examples of these in the accompanying diagram.)

Recall

Surprising though it may seem, research shows that we remember things best not immediately after committing something to memory but about ten minutes later, when the information has had time to 'settle'. After ten minutes there is rapid fall-off. We can counter the fall-off by spending a short time reviewing the material at this point, which will fix the information for about twenty-four hours. At this time a further review is necessary. The memory will then retain the information for about a week, when once again you need to review the material. After that only occasional reviews are needed for the material to remain permanently in the memory.

(continued)

The form of the review is also important. You need to be in a relaxed state. You can help yourself relax by sitting with your legs uncrossed, your feet firmly on the ground, your back vertical and your shoulders down. Many people find that quiet background music helps. Between your initial memorising and the first review (after ten minutes) you may well find it difficult to clear your mind of what you've been working on. Try to relax, as suggested above, for five minutes, then do some kind of physical exercise that forces you to concentrate on something else. If you are alone, stretching exercises are a good idea. If you are working with others, e.g. in class, a game involving physical movement is best.

As for the review itself, don't just look over your notes again. It will be much more effective if you put in more effort, using a three-phase sequence.

- Recall   Take a sheet of paper and write down as much as you can remember – this clarifies what you've remembered and what you've forgotten.

- Add   Go back to your original notes and add to your new notes whatever is missing – the small effort of copying will help you to remember the next time.

- Re-memorise   Try again to memorise specifically the items that escaped you earlier.

Cranmer *Motivating High Level Learners*
© Addison Wesley Longman Limited 1996 Photocopiable

Worksheet for Activity 1.11

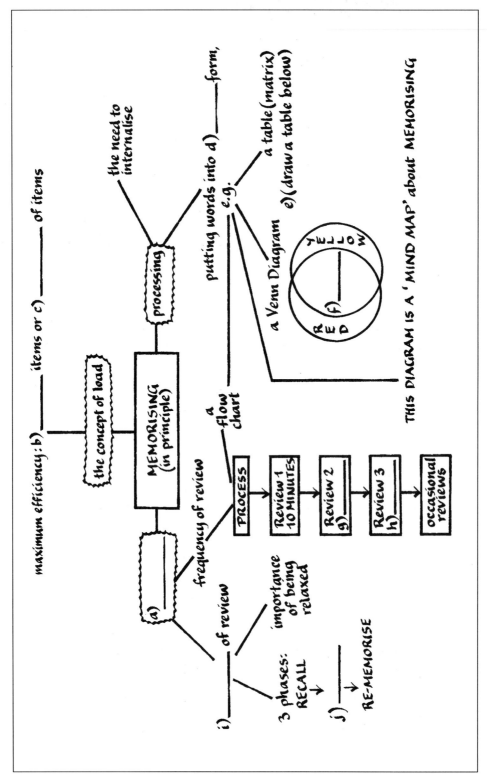

Cranmer *Motivating High Level Learners*
© Addison Wesley Longman Limited 1996

Fig. 6

'THE HALF IS GREATER THAN THE WHOLE'

FOCUS
Applying the principles of memorising: memorising when to use *do* and *make*

There are many pairs of words or structures in English which learners find hard to distinguish (for example, the difference between *do* and *make*, and whether a given verb is followed by a gerund or an infinitive). Books normally try to resolve the confusion by showing the use of both for students to learn. This activity shows a much easier and more efficient way of dealing with areas of this kind.

Do this activity as soon as possible after Activity 1.11 *Principles of memorising*, preferably the following lesson. If you have lessons of more than fifty minutes, do this activity in the last forty to fifty minutes.

MATERIALS
A class set of the Handout 'Expressions with *do*'

Preparation

Make a class set of the list of expressions with *do* on page 31. Alternatively, you could write the expressions on the board for your students to copy.

TIME
40–50 minutes

Procedure

1 Remind your students of some of the pairs of words/structures that tend to get confused. Tell them you are going to work with them on one such pair: *do* and *make*.

2 Tell the class that there is a fundamental principle to observe whenever there are two words/structures causing confusion: concentrate on just one of them. If, for example, they try to learn one list of verbs followed by gerunds and another of verbs followed by infinitives, they are likely to increase the confusion as they forget which verb was in which list. But if they learn only the list of verbs followed by gerunds, then a verb that is not on this list (apart from those few verbs that can take both and in any case need special treatment) must be followed by an infinitive. Learning only one list has two advantages. Firstly, there is only half the work involved in learning two. Secondly, in almost every case one of the pair is used significantly less than the other (e.g. there are rather fewer verbs that are followed by a gerund than there are followed by an infinitive). It makes sense therefore just to learn the shorter list, reducing the work still further.

3 Remind your class of the difference between the main meanings of *do* and *make* – that *make* gives the idea of creating or constructing, e.g. a cake, a model, a log fire, while *do* gives a more general idea of action or is used as an auxiliary verb.

4 Give out the copies of the list of expressions with *do* on page 31 or write them on the board. Check that students understand the meanings. Ask them to count how many expressions there are. (There are thirty-two.) Tell them that you are not giving them a corresponding list of expressions with *make* since there are at least sixty.

5 Elicit from your students the main points you covered in the lesson on memorising in principle (Activity 1.11): that the memory is most efficient when working with between five and nine items or groups of items, that a visual layout helps the process of memorising, that they need to do recall exercises in a particular way at specific intervals. Tell them you are going to work with them to apply these principles to memorising the expressions with *do*.

6 Instruct your students to work alone and divide the list up into groups of up to nine expressions, using whatever criteria they wish. Tell them to copy the groups of expressions out onto a blank sheet of paper and to spread them out visually on the page. Refer back to the diagram the students completed in Activity 1.11 as an example of information laid out visually. While they do this, monitor the class carefully. If you find a student maintaining groups of more than nine expressions, make them subdivide the groups. If they are maintaining a very linear layout, insist that they spread the groups out more visually. You will find that most students want to divide the expressions into semantic groups, though some prefer instead, or as well, to divide them phonologically. It doesn't matter what system they use so long as there is one, which means that processing the expressions will take place.

7 When your students have finished, give them about ten minutes to try to memorise their diagram.

8 Ask them to put their diagrams away and try to think of anything but the expressions for the next ten minutes. Tell them that they are going to spend five minutes relaxing and five minutes doing an activity that involves physical movement. (If the first five minutes don't distract them, the second five certainly will.) Ask them to find a comfortable position in their chairs (as described in the text on memorising in Activity 1.11). Suggest they close their eyes. If possible, put on about five minutes' worth of quiet, relaxing music – my favourite for this is any of Erik Satie's *Gymnopédies*, but harp or classical guitar music is also good, as is slow Baroque orchestral music. When the music finishes, bring everyone gently back to earth.

9 Choose one of the following activities, according to the ages/personalities of the members of your class and the space available.

a 'What's the time, Mister Wolf?' is a good game to try. Clear a large space in front of the board. Mr Wolf (you, the first time) stands facing the board. Everyone else lines up at a 'starting line' at the back of the space, as far away from Mr Wolf as possible. The class asks in chorus 'What's the time, Mister Wolf?'. Mr Wolf says a clock time, e.g. three o'clock/quarter to seven/ten past nine, and then the class advances one pace. Again they ask 'What's the time, Mister Wolf?'. Mr Wolf answers again and they take another pace forwards . . . and so on until he says 'Dinner time!', turns round fast and tries to catch one of the others, who try to run back to the starting line. If Mr Wolf succeeds, the person caught 'for dinner' becomes Mr Wolf and the previous one joins everyone else. If he doesn't succeed, he continues as Mr Wolf. After explaining the rules, play the game. (Be warned that the chasing phase is noisy for the teacher teaching in a classroom below or near yours.) The game continues, in this instance, for five minutes. Then sit everyone down again.

b For something quieter, try a trust game, e.g. 'The blind leading the blind'. Divide the class into pairs. If there is an odd one left over, you make up the pair. One student stands with his/her back to the other, eyes closed. The other stands behind and puts his/her hands on the front of the other one's shoulders. Like this they go for a walk, the back student being, as it were the front one's eyes. Do this for about two minutes, then reverse roles. (Some students get a little anxious in this activity, but many have told me how relaxing they find it.)

c If you're short of space, try some exercises sitting down. Sit at the front where everyone can see you and the way you move. Do the following sequence of exercises, at the same time instructing the class what to do.

● Begin by stretching, as you might when you get up in the morning.

● Make circular movements with your shoulders, first from back to front, then from front to back. Do this five times each way.

● Swing your head gently backwards and forwards, twice, then from side to side twice. Revolve your head slowly and gently, stretching your neck – do one revolution in one direction, then another in the opposite direction. Repeat these two revolutions.

● Wave your arms up and down five times as if you were flying. Put your arms out in front of you. Keeping your arms still, wave your hands gently up and down five times. Then revolve your hands five times from your wrists, first anticlockwise, then clockwise. Clench your fists, then stretch your fingers. Do this five times. Bring your arms and hands to rest.

● Stretch out your legs in front of you. Raise them and lower them five times. Keeping your legs stretched out in front of you, wave your feet gently up and down five times. Then revolve them five times from your ankles, first anticlockwise, then clockwise. Bring your feet to rest on the ground.

10 Get everyone to take out a piece of paper. Ask them, without referring to their diagrams, to write out on the paper as many of the expressions with *do* as they can remember. They can lay the expressions out in any way they wish. Allow up to five minutes for this. When they have reached their limit, tell them to refer back to their original diagram and add any they have missed to the new list. (In my experience this phase is unnecessary for about a third of the students – their recall is complete.) Give those who need it two to three minutes for re-memorisation of the expressions they could not recall. Then remind everyone that they must do a similar recall, add and re-memorise exercise after twenty-four hours, a week and thereafter from time to time. If you are able to do this in class, all well and good, but otherwise they must do it for themselves in their own time.

11 If you can find an exercise where the students have to choose between *do* and *make*, do it now. Your students will race through it, getting all the answers right. This not only shows the efficacy of the technique but leaves the students feeling really good.

NOTES

a I have noticed many times that the students who manage best to remember the expressions are those who have done a thorough job of dividing them into clearly-defined groups and have thought about the layout on the page, in Step 6.

b The technique of learning only one of two frequently confused sets of items also works well not only with gerunds and infinitives (learn just the gerunds), but also with prepositions that follow certain verbs and adjectives, e.g. *of* and *from* (learn *from*), *on* and *in* (learn *in*), *at* and *to* (learn *at*).

c This memorisation technique works well for learning other sets of words, e.g. irregular verbs (where the processing is often fascinating to students as they discover that, after all, there are many recurring patterns). A set as extensive as irregular verbs is too big to learn in one session. I normally work on it with students over a series of about five lessons – two for processing, three for memorising different groups of verbs.

HANDOUT FOR ACTIVITY 1.12

Expressions with *do*

an assignment	an injury
better	the ironing
one's best	a job
business	justice (to)
chores	a kindness (to)
the cooking	an operation
damage	repairs
the drying up	right
one's duty	a service (to)
evil	the shopping
an exercise	the washing (up)
a favour	wonders
good	work
harm	worse
homework	one's worst
the housework	wrong

CHAPTER 2

Noticing

'I know a bank whereon the wild thyme blows,
Where oxlips and the nodding violet grows
Quite overcanopied with luscious woodbine,
With sweet musk-roses, and with eglantine.'*
William Shakespeare

If we notice nothing, we have nothing to talk or write about. If we have nothing to talk or write about we cannot learn to do so in another language. This chapter provides opportunities of all kinds to notice and learn about people, places and things around us.

2.1

FOCUS
Noticing language

MATERIALS
Multiple copies of a text of your choice;
OHP and transparency (optional)

TIME
30–50 minutes initially

SO THAT'S HOW YOU SAY IT

Preparation

Choose a text of between 500 and 1000 words without too much new vocabulary (possibly one already used in class) but which contains language points that are worth your students noticing – particular uses of verb forms, prepositions, articles, collocations, idioms, etc. It is important to find one in a textbook of which you have multiple copies available, so that you don't risk infringing copyright.

If you have an OHP available, copy the checklist of language points mentioned in Step 4 onto an OHP transparency.

Procedure

1 Give out the text. Tell your students to read it through and note down any vocabulary they are unsure of. When they have done that, explain the vocabulary to them.
2 Tell them to read the text a second time and make a list of anything new to them that they would like to remember, so that they can use it later on in their own English. Suggest that they might notice phrases that they would never have thought of to express a particular idea. Point out that there may be certain structures that they may not be fully familiar with. Give them ten minutes working alone and then put them into pairs for a further ten minutes to compare what they have found and then jointly look for more items.

---

*thyme, oxlip, violet, woodbine, musk-rose and eglantine are all names of wild flowers.

3 Go through what they have found with the whole class and add any other points you think are important for them to notice.

4 Tell them to bring a similar-length text next lesson that they feel would also serve as a useful model for their colleagues. Project, or write on the board, the following list of the kinds of things they might be looking for. Talk them through this list giving examples so that they are clear what the terminology means:

Checklist of language items to look out for
1 use of articles
2 use of prepositions after verbs and adjectives, and in other contexts
3 use of verb forms
4 word order
5 false friends
6 useful vocabulary, including connectors
7 collocations
8 useful idioms
9 spelling
10 conventions of punctuation and layout

5 Next lesson put the class into pairs/threes. Get your students to show their partner(s) their text and the features of it they felt were useful. Tell them to discuss these features and ask you if there is anything they don't understand.

6 Tell them that it is obviously important to notice how native speakers express things when they speak and write, as languages are so vast that many small elements may never be focused on in class. On the other hand, make the point that they cannot realistically go into such detail all the time when listening to or reading something much longer.

NOTE
Repeat Steps 4 and 5 from time to time in order to remind your students of the importance of noticing language points for themselves.

2.2

FOCUS
Discussion on
reading outside
class

MATERIALS
Photocopies of
the Handout
'Guide to
choosing and
reading books'

TIME
30–40 minutes
(for Steps 1 to 5)

ENCOURAGING READING

One of the main characteristics of most successful advanced students is that they read regularly out of class, not just books for their studies but out of choice. This activity provides a framework for discussing this good habit and setting up a mechanism that encourages regular reading for pleasure. Do this activity early in a course, though I prefer to let a class settle a little first and do it around the fourth or fifth lesson. If you have a class of mature students with already well-established reading habits, you can prune this activity and just do Steps 1, 4 and 8.

Procedure

1 Initiate an informal discussion on your students' reading habits in their own language(s). Ask which of them are in the habit of reading regularly in English outside class. Ask what kind of things they read and where they get their reading material from.

2 Put it to the class that for most learners regular reading out of class is absolutely essential to reach an advanced language level – it is one of the best ways of expanding vocabulary and probably the only way to get a good sense of style. Tell them you are going to work with them to set up a framework that encourages them to read regularly.

3 The first hurdle is to find a source of suitable books. With the help of your students, write a list on the board of possible sources of books in English. Tell them to copy it into their notebooks. It will probably look something like this:

   a public lending libraries, including (overseas) British Council libraries
   b school/university/college libraries
   c class library – if each student contributes one or two books, the class immediately has a stock of books to read
   d bookshops
   e each other (by borrowing/exchanging)

   Discuss with the class which of these sources is/are most readily available.

4 Give out copies of the 'Guide to choosing and reading books' on pages 36–7. Ask them to read it and deal with the True/False statements at the end. Go through the answers with them.
   (2 is true; 1, 3, 4 and 5 are false; 6 is broadly true but also debatable to an extent – discuss this with the class.)

5 Arrange with your students for all to bring a book to class the lesson after next (unless you can take the class to a library on the premises, it is rarely realistic to insist on next lesson), so that everyone can get an idea of what their colleagues are going to read.

6 When the class bring their books, ask each student to set a realistic target date to read their book by. Tell them that the date must

be agreed with you. Draw up a class list of author/title/target date for all their books and fix this to the classroom wall.

7 As target dates are reached, check on progress. Don't be 'heavy' if they don't achieve their targets but remind them that they are the ones who set the target dates and that you do expect them to finish soon.

8 As students finish their books, ask them to fill in information about the books they have read on a 'book recommendation sheet', which you can fix to the wall for your students to consult. It might look like this:

RECOMMENDED READING

Author	Title	Interest	Difficulty	Comments	Reader

For 'Interest' and 'Difficulty' it is best to use a scale, e.g. one to five, to indicate the degree of interest and difficulty.

VARIATION

The same broad principles apply to listening. Below is a list of possible sources for material:

a English-speaking people that students meet
b television programmes, including satellite/cable TV
c films (original or subtitled, but not dubbed) in the cinemas and on television, film clubs, The British Council and other English-speaking cultural bodies
d videos (original or subtitled, but not dubbed)
e theatre, including companies touring overseas, locally-based English-speaking theatre in other countries
f radio, including BBC World Service
g songs
h spoken word cassettes

Discuss with your students which of these are available locally. Draw their attention to the help that images give in understanding and to the high level of concentration needed when listening, which is quickly tiring.

Follow-ups for listening are more difficult to set up than for reading. Once again, in general encourage reflection. Here are possible headings for a 'recommended listening sheet' that you can fix to the classroom wall:

RECOMMENDED LISTENING

Film/ Programme	Where/When seen/heard	Interest	Difficulty	Comments	Viewer/ Listener

ACKNOWLEDGEMENTS
Some of the ideas in 'Choosing a book for yourself' have arisen from discussion with colleagues, especially David Hardisty. The class book recommendations sheet idea has been in use for several years at the British Council, Lisbon. I have been unable to ascertain who first thought of it.

HANDOUT FOR ACTIVITY 2.2

Guide to choosing and reading books

a *Choosing a book for yourself*
1 You don't have to read 'Literature', you don't have to read novels. Choose something you will enjoy reading, fiction or non-fiction.
2 Try to vary the type of book you read, i.e. not always by the same author, not always on the same subject.
3 Don't choose something too long. If you are not yet in the habit of reading a lot, choose something of less than 200 pages. A collection of short stories is a good way to start.
4 Don't choose something too difficult. Most of what you read you should be able to understand without difficulty. If you constantly need the dictionary, reading becomes study, not enjoyment.
5 Before deciding to read a book, examine the first page. Is it the right level of difficulty for you? Does it make you want to read on? Is there anything in it you feel you can relate to? Do you like the style? If the first page does not satisfy you, don't be afraid to change your mind and choose another book.

b *Recommendations*
1 Your teacher may be able to suggest books that are available and suited to your level and interests.
2 Your colleagues, particularly if they are in the habit of reading, can tell you what books they have specially enjoyed reading.
3 Remember, though, you are the best judge of what is suitable for you, provided you choose with care.

c *While reading*
1 Try to set aside a regular time for reading. Just before going to bed at night is a good time. For some people the lunch hour is also good.
2 If after reading a number of pages you find you are not enjoying it, don't be stubborn. Give it up and find another book.
3 Sometimes some of the information contained in a book is hard to remember, e.g. relationships between characters in a novel, people and dates in a biography. You may find it helpful to make very brief notes. This is best done on a blank card, which you can also use as a bookmark.

d *After reading*
Reflect briefly on how much you enjoyed the book and why, whether it was easy or difficult to read and why (content/style/vocabulary), and whether you would recommend it to colleagues.

(continued)

True/False?
Which of these statements are true? Correct the false ones.

	T/F
1 Read good books such as literature.	☐
....	
2 Don't read very long books.	☐
....	
3 The more new vocabulary, the better.	☐
....	
4 It is best to read books recommended by others.	☐
....	
5 Take detailed notes on any book you read.	☐
....	
6 The aim of this type of reading is primarily pleasure.	☐
....	

Cranmer *Motivating High Level Learners*
© Addison Wesley Longman Limited 1996   Photocopiable

2.3

FOCUS
Raising student
awareness about
English as a *world*
language

MATERIALS
None

TIME
40 minutes in
class

A PROJECT ON AN ENGLISH-SPEAKING COUNTRY

While students recognise that English is spoken in Britain, the United States and, probably, Australia, New Zealand, South Africa, Ireland and Canada, they are rarely fully aware of the extent that it is spoken throughout the world. This activity aims to raise that awareness and asks them to find out about a less obvious English-speaking country in greater depth.

Procedure

1 Divide the class into pairs. Ask the pairs to draw up a list of English-speaking countries, that is to say, countries where English is an official language or is widely spoken. Be available to help supply the names of countries in English.

2 On the board draw five columns and head them with the names of the main continents (I always head the first column with the name of whichever continent I'm in). Ask your students for the names of the countries they wrote down in Step 1 and write them in the appropriate column. When you have exhausted their lists, add any others you feel they should know. The main countries are:

Europe:	Cyprus, Gibraltar (be sensitive about this, especially if you are in Spain), Ireland, Malta, The United Kingdom (be sensitive about the issue of Northern Ireland)
Africa:	Botswana, The Gambia, Ghana, Kenya, Lesotho, Liberia, Malawi, Namibia, Nigeria, Sierra Leone, South Africa, Swaziland, Tanzania, Uganda, Zambia, Zimbabwe
Asia:	Bangladesh, Brunei, Hong Kong, India, Malaysia, Pakistan, Singapore, Sri Lanka
Australasia and the Pacific:	Australia, Fiji, New Zealand, Tonga
The Americas:	Canada, The United States, Belize, many of the Caribbean islands, including The Bahamas, Barbados, Dominica, Grenada, Jamaica, Puerto Rico, St Lucia, St Vincent, Trinidad and Tobago, Guyana, the Falkland Islands (be sensitive about this if you are in a Spanish-speaking country, especially Argentina)

There are many more islands and island groups. Decide how exhaustive you wish to be and, accordingly, add them or not.

3 Explain to the class that you want them to do a project on one of these countries but not on England or the United States. (I exclude these two as they receive considerable coverage in coursebooks – I do allow Wales, Scotland or Northern Ireland, which are often neglected.) Tell the class to form groups of three or four. Let your students choose their partners, while making sure no individuals get left out. Ask each group to choose a country. I allow more than one group to work on the same country –

they often use quite different approaches and present interestingly different work – but you may decide you want your students to work on as broad a range of countries as possible, in which case they should all choose different countries.

4 When your students have chosen their countries, ask each group, for your reference, to give you a piece of paper with the names of the members in their group and which country they are going to work on.

5 Establish with the class the following:

   a how much you want each student to contribute to the project – I suggest about one thousand words.

   b the content – I set an upper limit of one third dedicated to the general background (geography and history, currency, industries, etc.) and insist that the greater part should be dedicated to the use of the English language, e.g. the role of English (as an official language, a *lingua franca*, etc.), how it differs from standard British/American English, periodicals published in English, literature, and so on. The possible areas of focus here vary considerably from country to country and you may need to discuss with each group those areas that would offer the most potential, e.g. the question of language variety is more appropriate where most or all of the population is English-speaking, the periodicals published in English are more relevant where English is one of the many languages used in the country.

   c the deadline by which the project must be handed in.

6 Discuss with your students what sources of information they are going to use. My students have worked principally from five sources:

   a encyclopedia entries, including those from CD-ROM encyclopedias, such as *Encarta*, *Grolier*

   b books

   c newspaper and magazine articles

   d computer programs, such as *PC Globe*

   e information from embassies, high commissions (the name for embassies in British Commonwealth countries) and tourist offices – the London telephone directory gives addresses and telephone/telefax numbers for London offices

You may be able to provide support from material you yourself possess – this is where it is useful to have a list of groups and their countries, so that you know who to give it to.

VARIATION

If you have time for this variation, it has the advantage of preparing and motivating the students better for the project. However, although it is very stimulating for many of them, it is also rather time-consuming.

1 Do Steps 1 and 2 early in the course in one lesson.

2 Present three or four different countries, each from a different continent, dedicating one or more lessons to each country. With one class, for example, I worked on India, Nigeria and Jamaica. With each country follow a regular pattern as follows:

    a In one lesson elicit from the class what they know about the country – I divide this into geographical features, language(s) and regions, history, literature and other aspects of culture, famous people, other points.

    b In the same lesson work on a text about the country, e.g. a recent newspaper article, so that your students know something about its present state.

    c In another lesson (or two) read a short story and/or poems by authors from that country, helping the students to appreciate what they read, especially as regards cultural information, but not going into details of literary criticism.

3 In another lesson set up the project as in Steps 3 to 6 above.

NOTES

a My students rarely achieve the one-third general, two-thirds English-language-related balance of contents. Nevertheless, demanding this kind of balance serves to focus their attention on the English-language aspects of the country, which is the purpose of the exercise.

b Assessment of projects of this kind, where this is necessary, is difficult. Some students, for example, lift passages wholesale from their sources, even if told not to, while others try to compose a text of their own. This makes linguistic assessment particularly difficult. Since the purpose of the project is primarily a cultural one, I do not make a big issue of the language aspect, but you must decide on your own policy in this regard, according to the assessment demands, if any, of your own teaching context.

c The information available and the extent and type of support from embassies, high commissions and tourist offices are very variable, giving some groups a plethora of information and others a dearth. India, because of its size and cultural wealth is an instantly attractive choice, but experience leads me to feel it is not ideal as students find themselves overwhelmed by the mass of information available and tend to fall down in their handling of it. Nigeria, on the other hand, raises some of the same issues but has proved to be more manageable.

ACKNOWLEDGEMENTS
I would like to thank the staff of various embassies and tourist offices in Lisbon for their assistance to my students, in particular the Embassies of Canada, Nigeria, Pakistan and South Africa for their exceptional care and support. This activity owes a great deal to joint planning and discussion with David Hardisty.

CULTURE PROJECT

Language is just one manifestation of a culture. Learning about other aspects of a culture is very motivating towards the learning of the language of that culture. This activity aims to set up 'culture projects' according to areas of interest to the students.

Procedure

1 Initiate a discussion with your students about their interests. Ask them about how they might link those interests to their study of English. Put it to them that they could extend an interest or begin a new one by doing a project on some aspect of English-speaking culture. Tell them that they can choose anything they like within that, only that at the end of the project they must produce something to present to the others in the class – orally or in writing. This can be something quite modest as its purpose is simply to provide some kind of objective. If you get a reasonably positive response, go on to Step 2. If you feel strong opposition to the idea, abandon it . . . at least, for the time being.

2 Tell them that the hardest part is often choosing the project. So give them copies of the handout on page 42. Ask your students each to decide on their project to tell you next lesson.

3 Next lesson ask each student what their project is going to be about and make a note of it. If more than one wants to work on a particular area, suggest they work in a pair, but discourage more than two students working on any one project. There are so many to choose from it is a pity not to have a wide range. Agree a target date for completion of the project and presentation to the class – in a one-month course it will have to be near the end of the course, in a year-long course towards the end of the term you start the project in. Tell your students that you will ask them from time to time how their projects are going and will set aside some class time to discuss progress and to deal with any problems.

VARIATION

I have had great success with mini-projects, where the students identify some small thing about English-speaking culture they want to know about and have just one lesson in a library to find out. You accompany them to the library and help them find the materials they need. The next lesson they report back what they found. Among mini-projects my students have chosen are: willow-pattern pottery, Shakespeare's life, the historical King Arthur, prehistoric monuments in Britain, Elgar, Liverpool and child labour in Victorian England.

ACKNOWLEDGEMENT
I owe the example topic 'ways of being' to Dianne Kiefer-Dicks (1993).

2.4

FOCUS
Encouraging identification with the target-language culture

MATERIALS
Photocopies of the Handout 'Example topics for personal culture projects'

TIME
10–20 minutes (Steps 1 and 2)

HANDOUT FOR ACTIVITY 2.4

Example topics for personal culture projects

1 *History*
- a long period, e.g. the Elizabethan era, the Victorian era
- a short period, e.g. the American Civil War, Henry VIII and the Reformation
- an incident and the events surrounding it, e.g. the Spanish Armada, the Wall Street Crash

2 *Geography*
- a country you don't know about where English is spoken, e.g. one of the Caribbean or Pacific islands/archipelagos, Tristan da Cunha, Ascension Island
- a region or state in an English-speaking country, e.g. Florida, Wales, Queensland
- a city or town, e.g. Cambridge (England or USA), Stratford-upon-Avon, Auckland

3 *People and their work*
- statesmen and women, e.g. Gandhi (Mahatma or Indira), Churchill, Lincoln
- scientists, e.g. Newton, Darwin, Einstein
- artists of all kinds:
  musicians, e.g. The Beatles, Louis Armstrong, Elgar
  painters/sculptors/architects, e.g. Constable, Whistler, Henry Moore, Wren
  poets, e.g. Blake, Betjeman, Pound
  novelists, e.g. Henry James, Jane Austen, V. S. Naipaul
  playwrights, e.g. Shakespeare, Shaw, Stoppard
- entertainers, e.g. Charlie Chaplin, Fred Astaire, Marilyn Monroe
- individuals, e.g. Bede, Samuel Pepys, Dr Johnson, Bertrand Russell, Martin Luther King

4 *Other areas*
- traditions and customs, e.g. Punch and Judy, pancake races, Thanksgiving
- the Royal Family
- the 'Mother of Parliaments', other political institutions
- castles, stately homes and gardens
- folk music, especially in the Celtic traditions
- food and cooking (contrary to much popular belief, there are a lot of excellent dishes to be found in Britain, e.g. Lancashire hotpot, beef olives, jugged hare)
- porcelain and pottery, e.g. Wedgwood, Royal Doulton
- an English sports team
- ways of being, e.g. attitudes, norms, taboos, behaviours

NEWS PROJECT

This project aims to encourage an outward-enquiring attitude towards events in the world. Some students take to this easily, others resist strongly. A mechanism for overcoming student resistance is provided here. This project will take several months to complete, so you will need to plan well ahead how you wish to fit it in with other items in your syllabus.

Procedure

LESSON 1

1 Put it to your class that it is very difficult to talk or write about issues of current interest, particularly in the more sophisticated way needed at a more advanced level if we don't keep in touch with what is going on in the world. A good way of broadening our knowledge of world events is to follow a particular issue over a period of time. Suggest that this is what you would like to happen.

2 Explain how it should work. First, each member of the class must choose an issue to follow – this is dealt with in Step 3. They decide how long the project should last and during that time collect materials related to their issue and keep them in a file. At the end they have to do three things: give the class a brief (five-minute) oral presentation of what they learnt about their issue, write a brief report on the issue – how it has developed, how it stands at present and how it might develop in the future – and hand the report together with their materials file for you to comment on and for their colleagues to look through. At regular intervals during the project you will ask how they have been getting on and offer any advice or suggestions they feel they need. Get your students' agreement to the project (gentle coaxing and discussing worries openly should succeed) or take it no further.

3 If they agree to the idea of the project, show them a list of possible types of issue they could pursue. Project this list with the OHP or write it on the board:

a a process of liberalisation
b a war, a civil war, civil unrest
c a process of integration, e.g. a country's accession to an economic community
d a process of independence
e a power struggle through democratic means
f a famine
g a peace process
h the actions of a statesman or stateswoman you admire

Give your students a few minutes to think of a possible project, then tell them that you don't want a decision now, but you will return to the project in a week's time, by which time you want them to have decided.

2.5

FOCUS
Being awake to events in the world

MATERIALS
OHP and transparency for Step 3 (optional)

TIME
Lesson 1:
30 minutes;
Lesson 2:
10–30 minutes

LESSON 2

1 A week later return to the subject of the news project. Ask your students what projects they have decided to do. If necessary, project the list of possible areas on the OHP again. Make a note of who is going to do what. If more than one want to do the same project, this is fine. If more than three want to do the same project, encourage them to choose different topics so that there is a broader range of issues being followed in the class. If they are insistent, divide them into pairs or threes and encourage each pair/three to take a different aspect of the issue.

2 Discuss how long the project is to last. Three to six months is ideal so that the issue has time to develop. Give a clear target date, e.g. by deciding already when the oral presentations are to take place and when the report and file are to be handed in.

3 Discuss with the class where they might get the material from – which newspapers and magazines are available (if you are working outside an English-speaking country). Remind them that they can write brief reports for their files, based on what they have heard on the radio or seen on the television.

NOTES

a Lesson 2 will vary in length according to the number of students in your class. Similarly, the amount of time you need to allocate for the oral presentations will vary.

   In the case of both the oral presentations and the reports, don't make a lot of the correctness of the language used as this isn't the point of the exercise. Much more important is to evaluate the extent to which each student has got involved in their project and how this is reflected in the output.

b Among successful projects my students have done are: political change in the Ukraine, Iraq in the aftermath of the Gulf War, the rise of right-wing political groups in Europe and the liberation struggle in East Timor.

THE CLASSROOM

It is best to do this activity before Activities 2.7 to 2.11.

Procedure

1 Tell the class to think for a moment about the way they are sitting. Ask them to put their feet firmly on the ground about a foot (30 cm) apart, sit well back in their chairs so that their backs and lower legs are vertical and their thighs horizontal. Now ask them to place their hands palm-down on their thighs, with their fingers just behind their knees, and to bring their shoulders down to a relaxed position. You do the same throughout this sequence. You should all look like Fig.7. Tell them you are going to call this position 'base position'.

2 Ask your students to try to be aware of how they are feeling today. Tired? Energetic? In a good mood? Annoyed? Headachy? Feverish? Too hot? Too cold? Pause briefly to give them a chance to sense these things. Ask them to focus their attention on their chair. Is it comfortable? Too hard? Too soft? Too low? Too high? Tell them to breathe in gently. What can they smell? Pleasant? Unpleasant? Ask them to focus on the sensations inside their mouths. Can they taste anything? Is it dry? Are they thirsty? Once again pause briefly.

3 Tell your class to close their eyes and listen to the sounds around them for about half a minute. Do so yourself too. When the time is up, initiate a discussion about the things they heard – the sounds inside the room and those outside. In the course of conversation they will inevitably change position, so when you have finished ask them to return to base position – feet firmly on the ground, shoulders down.

4 Tell them to look around the room and notice what is there. Then ask them to choose one object and look at it more closely: its colour(s), shape(s), texture(s), how the light strikes it, anything else they notice. Allow two or three minutes for this. Divide the class into groups of four and ask them to describe their objects to one another.

5 Round off the activity with a class discussion about what they have been doing. What was the point of it? (Noticing things we tend to take for granted.) How did they feel as they did the tasks? What was the point of returning constantly to base position? (It is a relaxing position but also one that encourages alertness.)

2.6

FOCUS
Noticing objects that surround us day by day

MATERIALS
None

TIME
20 minutes

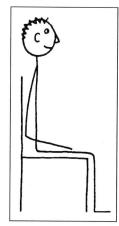
Fig. 7

2.7

FOCUS
Noticing trees,
flowers and
people's
behaviour

MATERIALS
A public park or
garden

TIME
90 minutes

PARKS AND GARDENS

It is best to do this activity after Activity 2.6. It involves a practical observation phase out of class, lasting about 45 minutes, with preparation and follow-up phases in class. According to your circumstances you may have to make special arrangements to do the practical phase with your class, or set it as a homework task.

Procedure

1 Work on vocabulary related to flowers and trees. Put the class into pairs and ask them to write down the names of parts of trees and flowers, non-specialist words. When they are ready ask what they wrote and draw up a list of tree-words and flower-words on the board. It might look something like this:

trees: trunk, branch, twig, leaf, blossom, bark, roots
flowers: leaves, flower (bloom), petal, stem, roots

2 Divide the class into two groups, A and B, and put them into pairs within the group. Instruct the class as follows:

GROUP A
Go to the park and look at the trees. With your partner make note of how many kinds there are and how to tell the difference between them. The names of the species don't matter. Spend about twenty minutes on this. Then discreetly and unobtrusively, observe the people in the park, in particular how they are sitting. Make a note of all the different positions people sit in, alone, with one other person, with a group of people. Again spend about twenty minutes.

GROUP B
Discreetly and unobtrusively, observe the people in the park, in particular the way they walk/move, when they are alone, with one other person, with a group of people. Does age make any difference? With your partner take a note of the different walks and ways of moving. Spend about twenty minutes on this. Then look at the flowers in the park. Decide how many different kinds there are and how to tell the difference between them. Spend another twenty minutes on this.

Unobtrusiveness and discretion are paramount, both so that the students do not make a nuisance of themselves and because it is important to observe people behaving spontaneously. That is why half the class looks at people first and the other half looks at them second.

3 After the visit to the park hold a feedback session. Ask the students who looked at trees to describe the different trees they saw. Be sure to move from pair to pair so that they all get a chance to report something back. Then do the same with the

flowers. With the ways of sitting and walking/moving ask them not only to describe but also to demonstrate – indeed in some cases this may be the only way to convey it. Throughout the feedback session, provide any help needed with vocabulary and write it on the board.

4 Ask the class what they feel they gained from this practical lesson. Usually they are struck by the sheer variety of everything, particularly in relation to the people.

NOTES

a If you are not teaching adults, check about your legal and insurance liability for lessons outside your teaching premises. Your students need to be old enough to work with only minimal supervision.

b If possible – it isn't always – do this activity yourself too, with the class. That way you can not only experience doing it but also benefit from the very positive effect it always has on the sense of togetherness in the class.

c Tessa Woodward describes a second cousin of this activity in her activity 'Jigsaw doing: using a nature trail' in *The Recipe Book* (Lindstromberg 1990), p. 67.

A VISIT TO THE MARKET

2.8

FOCUS
Vocabulary relating to markets; Shades of colour

It is best to do this activity after Activity 2.6. Like Activity 2.7 *Parks and gardens*, it involves a practical observation phase out of class with preparation and follow-up phases in class. You will probably need to make special arrangements to do the practical phase out of class – if necessary, set it as a homework task.

MATERIALS
A set of photographs of market scenes (optional); A market

Procedure

1 Divide your class into groups of five. Ask them to discuss, with the others in their group, markets they have been to, the kind of things they could buy there, the people buying and selling, the general atmosphere and anything else they think is important. Optionally, you can base this discussion around photos of market scenes: give some to each group. They discuss what is in each photo and then pass them on to another group to repeat the process, until all the photos have been round every group. This phase often makes students aware of their need for specific vocabulary, especially if you use photos, so supply any words they need.

TIME
Steps 1–4: 30–45 minutes; Steps 6–8: 30–45 minutes

2 If any language points arise in Step 1 that you think all the class should know, e.g. some of the vocabulary, draw everyone's attention to it now.

3 Describe the task you want them to do. You want everyone to visit

a market. If possible, arrange for the whole class to go with you. If this is not possible, your students will have to do this task by themselves or in smaller groups. Try to avoid busy times at the market, otherwise you risk making the students' presence unwelcome.

4 Tell the class to work in groups of five, the same as in Step 1 above. In each group, one student is to go to market and make a note of all the shades of green they can find, with the names of the item(s) that are that shade. For things they don't know how to say in English, they should ask the stall-keeper or a customer, if in an English-speaking country, otherwise note it in their own language to ask you next lesson. Another member of the group notes all the shades of red, another the shades of yellow, another the shades of brown, and another all the colours that are difficult to define.

5 Everyone visits the market.

6 Divide the class according to which colour they were working on at the market – greens, reds, yellows, browns and nondescript colours. Ask them to compare notes on the shades and items they found. They can add to or change their lists in the light of what other students found. Help with any vocabulary they need.

7 Draw up five columns on the board and label them *green, red, yellow, brown, nondescript colour*. Ask the members of the green group to come to the board in turn and write an item in the green column. They continue to do this till they have written up everything on their list. While they do so, you can explain any new vocabulary to the rest of the class. Ask the greens how they divided the various greens into shades. Did they agree or were there wide differences of opinion? Repeat this process with the other groups.

8 Show your class how English often uses the names of objects to define colours or shades of colours. Here are some examples of the linguistic means of doing this, taking objects you might easily find in a market:

a the name of the object plus the name of the colour, e.g. *pea green, lemon yellow*

b similes (especially for red), e.g. *as red as a cherry/beetroot/lobster*

c the object functioning as a colour, e.g. *orange, aubergine*

d the object plus *-coloured* (for things that are difficult to give a definite colour to), e.g. *pineapple-coloured*

Tell your students to experiment with these ways of making colour more precise in future compositions.

NOTES

a There are often cultural differences in the way different nationalities perceive what range of shades constitutes one colour. For example what in English is called 'brown' sugar is considered to be 'yellow' by the Portuguese and 'black' tea is considered to be 'red' in India. This activity can bring out these differences quite strikingly in classes with students of more diverse cultures.

b In terms of language work you miss nothing by making the visit to market an individual homework task. In terms of the dynamic of the class, you miss a golden opportunity to create or strengthen solidarity in the class.

c Some classes are very resistent to the 'class outing' approach to this activity. You need to deal with objections sympathetically but firmly. The first time I tried it, I warned the class well in advance that I had this in mind and was greeted with a round of groans. On my mentioning it a second time a week or so later, they came up with all kinds of practical reasons why it wouldn't work – some weren't sure where the market was, some didn't know how to get there, one mentioned a rumour of a transport strike. I dealt with all of these points. The lesson before I planned we should go, one said, 'It's a nice idea but I doubt if anyone will show up. I'll be there but I don't suppose most of the others will.' With the exception of the one who said this (who never appeared), all turned up punctually at half-past eight in the morning, had a really good time, wanted to do something similar soon and considered it one of their best lessons ever.

MY WAY TO WORK

2.9

FOCUS
Noticing things as we go about our daily business

MATERIALS
Photocopies of the two texts 'From home to work I and II'

TIME
30 minutes

It is better to do this activity after Activity 2.6. I often do it a few days after Activity 2.7 *Parks and gardens*, but it also works well as a later reinforcement. Make copies of the two texts on pages 51–2 and 53–4. One, written a few years ago, describes my walk to work as it was when I first did this activity. The second one, written recently, describes a very different journey to work, as it is at the time of making final revisions to this book.

Procedure

1 Remind your class about work they have already done on observing things, e.g. Activity 2.7 *Parks and gardens*. Tell them that today you are going to focus on the things we pass and the thoughts we have day after day without ever really noticing them.

2 Give out a copy each of the Handout 'From home to work I' on pages 51–2. Ask your students to read it and draw a circle round any words or phrases that describe things other than through the eyes, i.e. sounds, smells and physical sensations. Tell them not to worry about vocabulary they don't understand unless they feel it is preventing them from fulfilling the task, in which case they should ask you. Allow about five minutes for this. Discuss with them what they found.

3 Ask them to go through the text a second time and underline any

words they don't know. Go through the vocabulary, as far as possible eliciting the meaning of words from those students that do know it.

4 Divide the class into three groups. Now give each student a copy of the Handout 'From home to work II' on pages 53–4 and ask them to read it looking out for particular aspects of what it describes. Tell group one to draw a circle round any words or phrases describing things other than through the eyes, as in Step 2 above. Group two is to circle verbs of movement, group three the author's thoughts and feelings. Once again tell them not to worry about vocabulary unless it is preventing them from fulfilling the task. Allow about five minutes for this and then ask each group what they found within the category they were looking for.

5 As before, ask them to go through the text a second time, underlining any words they don't know. Then go through the vocabulary.

6 Ask your students what differences they find in the author's two treatments of his journey to work and invite them to suggest reasons for these different treatments. The group task in Step 4 draws attention to the principal differences, namely that the first text limits itself to describing the physical objects the author notices, while the second also lays emphasis on the people and his thoughts and feelings. The principal reason for the difference is that the first route is particularly scenic, while the second is much less so. However, it also reflects a choice on the author's part as to what to include and what to omit.

7 Set a composition (about 300 words, depending on the level of your class) asking your students to describe their way to work or school, making it as atmospheric as possible, and being sure to include senses other than sight. Warn them that this is a more difficult composition than it seems at first, in particular it is important actually to make the trip with the idea of doing the composition in mind and that they will need to be selective as to exactly what they include in their composition.

NOTE

Many of my students tell me how difficult they find the follow-up composition. However, they find the challenge very valuable and the whole experience very rewarding . . . and they often produce outstanding work even describing very dreary journeys.

HANDOUT 1 FOR ACTIVITY 2.9

From home to work I

My flat is on the first floor of an eighteenth-century building in one of the old quarters of Lisbon. As I leave it and walk down the street I pass other buildings of the same period, some with crumbling façades like my own, others restored and painted salmon-pink like many other buildings in the city.

I then go through the 'Feira da Ladra' or thieves' market, which on Tuesdays and Saturdays is busy and colourful but on other days empty and drab. Soon I come to the tramlines and the winding street down which the trams rattle towards the city centre.

I go straight across and up a rising street. At the brow of the rise there is a house on the left with wrought-iron balconies, a coat of arms above the door and glazed-tile panels on the walls. In bygone days it must have belonged to someone rich and noble.

I follow the street as it twists and turns until I reach a junction and more tramlines. The street here is cobbled with worn-out cobbles, smooth and rounded with gaps between, neglected for many years by the City Council street department.

I continue up the other side. It's uphill but it's not so bad when I think of the great relief I shall feel when I reach the top. Before long I reach a row of old houses with balconies and aged street lanterns. One of these houses has a particularly fine example of the typical doorknockers such as you find on many front doors – reaching out of a frilled cuff, a hand with a ring on the third or fourth finger, clutching a ball.

After a while I come to the top of some steps. As I go down I am aware of the little stones that make up the steps and the sensation in the soles of my feet as they go down the steps one by one. My hand feels the cold of the handrail that runs down the middle of the steps from top to bottom. I look up at the houses, the roof tops and city centre below. It looks so peaceful from here.

I make my way down narrow, twisting alleys and steps to the bottom. Here, so suddenly, it is busy with traffic. I hate this part of the walk – along and across streets full of cars and buses, motorbikes and lorries, each contributing a billow of fumes to the general filth of the air. Eventually I cross the black-and-white-patterned paving of one of the main squares before I reach

(continued)

the bottom of the funicular railway. If I'm lucky there's one waiting for me and not too many people in the queue. If I'm less lucky, which is more often the case than not, I have to walk up. I tell myself it's good for me as I set off slowly up the seemingly endless hill. On cold midwinter mornings I'm sweating like a pig when I reach the top, thanks to my thick Alentejo cape, which is designed for Siberian cold and weighs a ton. At the top I rest for a moment.

It's not much further now but still uphill. As I go on a little I look back over the city. It's a magnificent view, sometimes clear, sometimes shrouded in mist. Whichever is the case, it is magical and reminds me of my first day in Lisbon, when I saw this unforgettable view for the first time.

I pass the antique shops and cross the garden of Principe Real. On wet days the great shade tree wafts the perfume of juniper berries and leaves. I breathe in appreciatively as I admire the wealth and variety of trees and flowers and people there. In two minutes I will have crossed the park, past the bougainvillea-lined walls and winding streets, and into the Institute compound and the pink building where I give my classes.

Cranmer *Motivating High Level Learners*
© Addison Wesley Longman Limited 1996   Photocopiable

HANDOUT 2 FOR ACTIVITY 2.9

From home to work II

It is almost half past seven in the morning (but should be a quarter past seven – I'm late as usual) and it is still dark as I close the door of our flat and sleepily trudge down the two flights of stairs to the ground floor. I open the narrow street door and make my way outside.

The lights illuminate the houses of this part of Lisbon, known as the 'Bairro das Colónias' and built some sixty years ago when Portugal was a major colonial power. I cross over Rua de Moçambique (my street) and walk down Rua de Guiné in the middle of the road. There are few if any cars coming up at this time of day, and as the pavements turn into a treacherously slippery slope on damp or wet days, I've got into the habit of walking in the middle of the road. At the bottom of the street I meet other signs of life as others, equally sleepy and in just as much of a hurry as me, rush hither and thither to catch lifts, buses, taxis, underground trains, or just rush on foot. I cross the road at the traffic lights and descend to the 'metro'.

This underground station, unlike some of the others in Lisbon, is gloomy and miserable. The people waiting seem to add some of this gloom and misery to their tired faces. By now it is twenty-five to eight and I start to panic as the first train is not going on the branch line I want. Will I be late for work? (I never have been so far, but these irrational panics are no less felt for that.) As the next train comes grating along the lines and I prepare to board, I try to remember the best carriage to be in so that I'm right by the exit at the other end. In I get, greeted, as usual, by a wall of hot, stuffy air. With a bit of luck, I'll find a seat straight away, but if I don't, I will within a stop or two.

Sometimes I read a book or magazine, sometimes correct the latest batch of homework. Sometimes I don't have either with me or I just don't feel like being so active at what feels like the middle of the night. Then I enjoy the journey looking about me: a woman dressed up for work as if she were on her way to some very exclusive party; a young man asleep in a corner, still drunk from the evening before; two young girls chattering away and giggling on their way to school – the only real sign of life on the train. At each stop people go out and others come in, as if in some strange ritual of changing places. After fifteen minutes I am at my stop. Up I get and leave the train. I got it wrong again – the exit is much further along the platform than I had

Cranmer *Motivating High Level Learners*
© Addison Wesley Longman Limited 1996 *(continued)*

remembered. Slightly amused at such consistent incompetence, I plod up the stairs, take a free ride up the escalator, round the corner, up more stairs and out again, with relief, into the open air.

The weather here, nearly half an hour since I left home, is often surprisingly different – colder, mistier, wetter on a wet day, a more exposed spot with more extreme weather. I follow students along a short cut. On wet days it tends to be muddy, especially beneath a great pine tree beside the track. I continue to the way out, a gate in front of Lisbon's main hospital, the Santa Maria, and thread my way, often with difficulty, around the cars parked on the pavement. Crossing the road at that spot is fraught with difficulty as the cars come streaming in along this major highway into the city centre. The zebra crossing is the only chance, though few motorists take a blind bit of notice of it. I feel a sense of achievement as I reach the other side without having to be admitted to the Accident and Emergency unit of the hospital.

It is then downhill all the way, the hospital railings on one side, the busy road on the other. Another busy highway to cross, but with traffic lights there, which the motorists by and large observe, it is much easier to cross. The clock on an island in the middle of the road says two minutes to eight. By a hair's breadth, I shall be up the steps on the other side and into class at eight o'clock sharp. 'How annoyingly punctual the British are!' my students will remark.

Cranmer *Motivating High Level Learners*
© Addison Wesley Longman Limited 1996   Photocopiable

'FINE WEATHER FOR DUCKS'

2.10

It is better to do this activity after Activity 2.6. It is said that the British are always talking about the weather as it is so changeable in Britain. It is useful for learners to have a good knowledge of weather vocabulary not only because of this, but because they can use the weather and people's reactions to it to create atmosphere in descriptions and stories.

FOCUS
Noticing the weather and its effect on people

MATERIALS
None

TIME
45–75 minutes

Procedure

1 Introduce the topic *weather*. Tell your students that it is important to know how to describe the weather not only for its own sake but because making reference to it is often a good way to create a sense of atmosphere in a story. They can also make their characters react to the weather in the story.

2 On the board draw up seven columns, as follows:

hot   cold   wind/calm   storms   precipitation   cloud/sun   humidity

Divide the class into pairs and ask each pair to copy these headings and write in the appropriate column(s) any words they know related to weather. When they have written all they can think of, put the pairs together to make groups of four. Ask them to compare their lists and add any words that they missed. Make a class list on the board by asking for contributions from the different groups. Add any additional words you think your students should learn.

3 Introduce the subject of people's reaction to weather and how this varies from person to person. Ask your students to work by themselves (emphasise this) for a moment and make a note of how they feel in the following weather (write this list on the board):

a warm and sunny
b cold and dry
c hot and humid
d very hot and dry
e bitterly cold
f cold and wet
g mild and wet
h thunder and lightning

Put them into pairs to compare their reaction with their partner. Chair a class discussion of their reactions to the different kinds of weather.

4 Put pairs together to make groups of four. Write these questions on the board and ask them to discuss them:

How would you feel and look if
a you'd been out in the pouring rain without a coat or umbrella?
b you'd been out in the freezing cold with no coat, hat or gloves?
c you'd been out working in the boiling sun?
d you'd been out walking in a gale?

Chair a class discussion as a follow-up and introduce some of the more descriptive expressions that native speakers use, e.g.:

wet through, soaked to the skin, like a drowned rat, shivering, chattering, sweating like a pig, wind-swept, dishevelled

EXTENSION
Whenever there is a change in the weather, check with your students that they know how to describe it and if necessary add items to their list of weather words. Ask them how they feel about the new weather.

2.11

FOCUS
Eradicating banal vocabulary

MATERIALS
Photocopies of the Worksheets and Handout; OHP and transparency (optional)

TIME
50–90 minutes

'THAT'S NICE!'

It is better to do this activity after Activities 2.6 to 2.9. A common weakness among potentially advanced students is a tendency to play safe and work within the same limited range of structures and vocabulary. This activity draws attention to this problem in relation to vocabulary and provides opportunities to explore richer alternatives. Do it as a revision and extension of the observation activities in this chapter (Activities 2.6 to 2.9). If your lessons are of 50 minutes or less, do Steps 1 to 3 in one lesson and Step 4 in another.

Preparation

Make multiple copies (one for each student) of the Worksheets on page 59 and the Handout on page 60 (see Steps 3, 5 and 8). It is important in the Handout that the students edit the text between the lines. Prepare an OHP transparency of the guidance in Step 8.

Procedure

1 Write these two sentences on the board and invite comments on the differences:

a It was a nice day as he walked down the street.
b It was a still, sultry day as he hobbled, dripping with sweat, down the narrow, cobbled street.

Ask your students exactly where the differences occur – *nice* and *walked* are replaced by more evocative words, 'he' is described in terms of how he would feel in this weather (see Activity 2.10 *'Fine weather for ducks'*), the street is made more atmospheric (see Activity 2.9 *My way to work*). Ask the class which sentence they consider more appropriate coming from an advanced student and why. Suggest that the second sentence is the kind of writing they should be aiming at, even if they don't yet have a rich enough vocabulary.

2 Draw attention to the word *nice*. Tell the class that as of now you are going to ban this word from written work. (You can allow it in speech.) Tell them you are going to work with them on other, more precise or evocative words to use instead.

3 Put them into pairs and distribute Part 1 of the Worksheet on page 59. There are eight sentences and a 'cloud' containing eighteen adjectives. Ask your students to work in pairs and select one or more alternatives for *nice* in each sentence. Some of the alternatives can be used in several sentences.

4 When everyone has finished, go through their answers. This is very important as the learners often think they can use some of these words where they don't fit well.

5 Distribute copies of Part 2 of the Worksheet on page 59 (taken from work that students of mine have written). All contain the word *nice*. Ask each pair to imagine they were the partner of the student who wrote each sentence. What advice would they give as to how to improve the sentence by replacing *nice*?

6 While they are doing this, monitor the class carefully. They may want to use vocabulary that did not appear in Step 3 and may need your help. Again go through your students' answers when they have finished, not only to help delimit the use of alternatives, but also so that the pairs can see what other solutions their colleagues have found.

7 Sum up ways of making vocabulary less banal and more evocative.

8 Project the following on the OHP or write it on the board. Ask the class to copy it into their notebooks. (Don't give it out as a handout as I find it sinks in better if they copy it down themselves.)

To raise the level of your writing:
a Apply things you have observed where the context allows you to do this, e.g. colours and shapes, weather and people's reactions to it, ways people move, features of streets, gardens and so on.
b Avoid trivial words, especially *nice*, but also words like *walked* and *went*, where there are suitable, more evocative alternatives.

9 Give out copies of the simple story about Jack and Jill in the Handout on page 60. Ask your students to work in pairs to make it more evocative. Tell them to be selective as to the changes they make, following the guidelines you have just given them,

but without making changes and additions just for their own sake. The story should remain simple but with more striking, less commonplace vocabulary. They can write their changes in the spaces between the lines.

10 When everyone in the class has finished, chair a discussion of the changes the pairs have made.

NOTE

The word *interesting* is often used as a blanket to smother more precise or evocative words. At more advanced levels I like to ban it too.

ACKNOWLEDGEMENT

When I was at school, our teachers would not allow us to use the words *nice* or *lovely* in compositions. Nowadays I don't find *lovely* so objectionable but I agree wholeheartedly with banning *nice*.

WORKSHEET FOR ACTIVITY 2.11

Part 1

1 The weather was nice.

....

2 They had a nice time.

....

3 She's a nice woman.

....

4 There are some nice paintings in the exhibition.

....

5 What a nice dress!

....

6 I had a nice lunch.

....

7 I hope you'll have a nice holiday.

....

8 It's a nice book.

....

colourful
charming
sunny
exciting
pretty
kind
enjoyable
beautiful
warm
delicious
sweet
generous
bright
attractive
relaxing
exquisite
fascinating
delightful

Cranmer *Motivating High Level Learners*
© Addison Wesley Longman Limited 1996   Photocopiable

✂ -

WORKSHEET FOR ACTIVITY 2.11

Part 2

a The house was in South Kensington and the family was very nice.
b I've become more responsible and friendly, taller and nicer.
c How nice of you to introduce yourself in such a friendly letter.
d She isn't very fashionable but she looks nice.
e Talking about the class, I mean the other students in my class, I think they are nice.
f Have a nice trip.
g At this time of the year all the shops have got nice things.
h I would say I had a nice time at school.
i How wonderful it is to have a nice house.
j The inhabitants are very nice and friendly.
k The first impression of being away from home was not nice.
l In short, the movie was really nice.

Cranmer *Motivating High Level Learners*
© Addison Wesley Longman Limited 1996   Photocopiable

HANDOUT FOR ACTIVITY 2.11

Jack and Jill

It was a nice day as Jack and Jill left their small flat and walked down the street. Towards the bottom they saw an old lady crossing the street. Suddenly she fell. They went over to her and helped her up. She thanked them and gave them a coin to express her gratitude. They looked at the coin. On one side it said, 'Please turn over.' On the other it said, 'Whoever possesses this coin may have three wishes.' So Jack and Jill went into the park nearby and sat under a tree to think what their wishes would be.

'I don't know what we should wish,' said Jack, 'but I wish I could sit under this tree for ever and never have to work.' 'And I wish that I could sit here for ever beside you,' said Jill.

Some time later they still hadn't decided what to wish but wanted to leave. They tried to get up but couldn't. It was then that they remembered the wishes they had accidentally made.

'What shall we do?' asked Jack.

'Be a bit more careful with our last wish,' said Jill. 'I think we should wish to be as we were but a bit richer.' Jack agreed. So that is what they wished.

Now they live in a nice little cottage with a nice big garden, as content as could be.

CHAPTER 3

Imagination and creativity

'To see a World in a Grain of Sand
And a Heaven in a Wild Flower,
Hold Infinity in the palm of your hand
And Eternity in an hour.'
  William Blake

Everyone can imagine. Everyone can be creative. It's just a question of knowing how and letting yourself. This chapter shows you how. There is no excuse for dull writing.

THE LICENCE

Many people are afraid of their imagination. They are afraid that it is too wild, that they will be laughed at if they say what they really imagine. Some people consciously or unconsciously block their imagination because of this fear. A first step, therefore, in freeing the imagination is to give it permission to be. This activity is a first step in this direction, so do it as a preliminary to other work from this chapter.

Preparation

Make a photocopy of the 'Licence' on page 63 for each student. Make sure it is well centred on the page and if possible enlarge it to make it more impressive.

Procedure

1 Elicit from your students synonyms and near-synonyms for *crazy*. Write them on the board. Add a few yourself, including any that have not yet come up but which appear in the licence below. Some words, such as *nuts*, *bananas*, *bonkers* and *round the bend*, students find very amusing so teach some as this helps to set the right mood for this activity.
2 Chair a brief discussion about craziness, imagination and creativity. Ask your students if they find it easy to be imaginative and creative. If you yourself find it difficult, admit it and suggest where you think the difficulty lies. Talk with the class about difficulties

3.1

FOCUS
Allowing ourselves to be bizarre

MATERIALS
Photocopies of the 'Licence'; (Optional) Sealing wax/red candles and a lighter/ matches

TIME
15–20 minutes

they experience; with students who don't feel they have difficulties in this area, ask them for ideas that might help.

3 Tell the class you are going to be working with them using activities that encourage imagination and creativity, but before doing so, you want them all to have a licence to be as crazy as possible and to enjoy it.

4 Give out copies of the licence and ask your students to fill them in – full name, signature and date. Optionally, but strongly recommended, take in some sealing wax or some red candles and melt some on the bottom of each licence to make a seal. Your students can help you with this. Then get them to incise their initials in the soft wax, using a pencil or ballpoint pen.

NOTE

Beware of the fire risk in Step 4 if you take up the seal idea, especially if you have smoke detectors in your classroom. One student of mine wanted to char the edges of the licence to make it look old and therefore even more impressive. I think it's a wonderful idea but wouldn't risk it in class.

ACKNOWLEDGEMENT

This activity is inspired by the work of Eloise Ristad, in particular 'The Book of Judges' in *A Soprano on Her Head* (Ristad 1982).

I hereby give myself

_____

permission to say silly and bizarre things,

to write mad, crazy things,

to be totally and completely daft ...

and to enjoy every minute of it.

Signed _____

Date _____

Fig. 8

3.2

FOCUS
Adding
description to
narrative;
Encouraging
imagination

MATERIALS
None

TIME
50–80 minutes

BEAUTY AND THE BEAST

If we take a novel and analyse the proportion of narrative (where the verbs are past simple to portray events) and description (where, discounting sections of dialogue, the verbs are in other forms, or, if past simple, denote states or habits rather than events), we come to the conclusion that most novels have far more description in them than narrative. One way of drawing attention to this is to tell a bald narrative and get your students to add the descriptive detail.

Preparation

1 Take a story. Decide which elements you want your students to describe and at what points in the story. Bearing that in mind, reduce the story to a 'skeleton', indicating what you want described where (we will exemplify with 'Beauty and the Beast'):

● There was a merchant. (*Describe the merchant.*)

● He had three daughters: Ugly (the ugliest), Greedy (the greediest) and Beauty (the youngest and most beautiful). (*Describe Ugly, Greedy and Beauty in greater detail.*)

● The merchant's fortunes were declining. He wanted to travel to set up new business. He asked each daughter what he should bring back from his trip. Ugly wanted face creams and perfumes, Greedy wanted food and drink, Beauty wanted just a rose. The merchant went on his trip but didn't manage to set up any new business. On his way back he went past an apparently uninhabited palace surrounded by a garden. (*Describe the garden.*)

● In the garden were some roses, so the merchant stopped and picked a rose for Beauty. At that moment appeared the owner of the palace and garden, a monster. For stealing the rose, he threatened to kill the merchant unless he gave him Beauty. The merchant had no choice and agreed. When he got home he gave Beauty the rose and explained what had happened. Beauty agreed to go and live with the monster. Next day she went to meet the monster, who showed her round the palace. (*Describe the palace.*)

● After a while, Beauty grew to like the monster, who was very kind to her, and they decided to get married. On their wedding day, the monster suddenly turned into a handsome prince. So Beauty's goodness and courage were rewarded and they all lived happily ever after.

2 Memorise this skeleton.

Procedure

1 Tell your students to take a piece of paper and mark alternate lines with a dot, as you want them to write on alternate lines. Explain that you are going to tell them a story but that you want them to add the descriptive details from their imaginations.

2 Check that your students understand the words *merchant* and *greedy*, explaining them if necessary.

3 Tell them the first part of the story and then ask them to describe the merchant, writing their descriptions on alternate lines. Remind your students that you are telling the story in the past, so their descriptions must also be written in the past. While they are writing, be available to help with vocabulary needs. You may also want to take the opportunity to remind yourself of the next part of the story and/or write your own description. When you see that most students are finishing, ask the class to finish the sentence they are writing. After about half a minute (when you see your students are ready), continue with the next part of the story . . . and so on till the end of the story.

4 Ask your students to exchange their descriptions with a partner. (They will want to anyway, as they will be fascinated to know what their colleagues have written.) Tell them to mark any corrections that they think should be made in the space between the alternate lines.

5 Tell them to discuss the corrections with their partner and come to an agreement about whether the correction is justified. You can act as arbiter if they fail to agree.

VARIATION

If you use a well-known story, such as 'Beauty and the Beast', some of your students are likely to know it. After the final description, ask them between them to tell the end of the story to the rest of the class. Allow and encourage imaginative variations of the version(s) you know – a certain irreverence can be a lot of fun.

NOTES

a In the descriptions of the daughters, if you don't partially describe them yourself, along the lines suggested above, the students sometimes describe them in terms of the opposite of their name. This creates a dilemma later as to which accompanies the monster later in the story, a problem which I prefer to avoid in this way.

b In theory you could ask your students to describe the monster and the prince. With four descriptions of people at the beginning of the story, however, I find that their imagination fails and the class tends to get bored even describing the monster – Ugly and Greedy are already monstrous enough for most students to have used up their vocabulary in this area already.

c If you have to work within a fifty-minute lesson, set a time limit of four minutes for each description (therefore twelve minutes for the three sisters). Otherwise the correction phase will be very rushed.

ACKNOWLEDGEMENT
I first learnt this story-telling technique from *Once Upon a Time* (Morgan & Rinvolucri 1983). The story they use as an illustration is Thurber's 'The Unicorn in the Garden', which I have used many times with success.

<table>
<tr><td>

3.3

FOCUS
Stimulating the imagination

MATERIALS
None

TIME
30–40 minutes

</td><td>

IF A TABLE COULD SPEAK ...

If possible remove all furniture and other obstacles between your students and the board. Sometimes it is easiest to do this by moving the students to the front of the classroom. I like to do this activity early in a course as it has a very good effect on the sense of group and fun in the class.

Procedure

1 Draw an object, e.g. a table, on the board (however well or badly). Tell the students that your object is the starting point for a picture you would like the class to create and that you would like them to come up to the board one at a time and add more things to it. Tell them that they can draw absolutely anything except people and that the quality of the drawing doesn't matter. The picture is finished when there are about a dozen items in it.

2 Put the chalk or board pen where everyone can reach it easily – make sure they know where it is. Then get out of the way and let them draw the picture.

3 When the picture is reasonably complete, i.e. when there are about a dozen items in it, declare the picture ready. (See Fig. 9 for an example of a completed picture built around a table.) If your class has had to come out to the front, send them back to their usual places.

4 Divide the class into pairs. Ask the pairs to choose any two items in the picture, e.g. the table and the plant in Fig. 9, and write a dialogue between them of about ten lines. Tell your students they must not mention the names of their items in the dialogue. For example, if it is a dialogue between the table and the plant, the plant mustn't say, 'Hello, table! How are you today?' but just, 'Hello! How are you today?' Give a time limit of fifteen minutes (but be prepared to allow up to twenty). First reaction to this task is usually a gasp of shock, but they quickly get used to the idea. Keep well out of the way – I often leave the room completely – for about five minutes while they settle. Then be available to help

</td></tr>
</table>

Fig. 9

with vocabulary, etc. If you're not needed, don't hover, just sit down out of the way. As they are finishing, go round and check they have not mentioned the names of the 'speakers' in their dialogue as this will ruin Step 5.

5 When they have finished, ask the pairs in turn to read aloud their dialogue, each partner taking a part. The others in the class must guess which item is talking to which. This phase is very good for making students read loud and clearly as colleagues will not otherwise understand.

NOTES

a Sometimes there are lulls between students going up to the board to add to the picture. When this happens it is difficult, as a teacher, not to intervene by adding something yourself. You mustn't. If necessary, make some encouraging comment like 'Would somebody else like to add something?' Situations of this kind can become something of a test of the teacher's nerves, but to be fully successful the activity depends on the active participation of as many members of the class as possible and minimal teacher intervention.

b The lack of human beings in the picture is important as it is more of a challenge to the imagination, and frankly much more fun. One of the best dialogues I have come across was between a window and a curtain – in a curious way it was very profound and psychologically penetrating.

c Other good starting objects are a tree, a lamp, a grandfather clock.

ACKNOWLEDGEMENT

I described a similar version of this activity as 'Creative picture dialogue' in *More Recipes for Tired Teachers* (Sion 1991). The idea of the collective picture is taken from *Once Upon a Time* (Morgan and Rinvolucri 1983).

3.4

FOCUS
Imagining
ourselves in
someone else's
shoes;
Revision of
question forms

MATERIALS
Several postcards
or a poster/slide
of a painting;
Slide projector
(optional)

TIME
20–40 minutes

PEOPLE IN PAINTINGS

You can use paintings not only while working on the topic of art but with whatever theme is portrayed in the painting. The detailed steps involved in this activity depend on the painting you use, but the technique is always centred around writing questions to ask the main character or characters in the painting and answering in the role of the character(s). Great care is needed in the choice of painting. It must focus on one or a small number of people and there must be a strong sense of stillness, of capturing a split second, in the painting. I am illustrating the technique with three famous and contrasting paintings to give you an idea of the range and type of paintings you can use and how the treatment needs to vary.

Preparation

1 Obtain enough postcards of the painting you are going to work on for at least one per three students. I like to keep sets of at least a dozen. Alternatively you can use a poster or slide and slide projector so that all the class can see the painting at once. To obtain postcards, posters or slides of the paintings reproduced here, you need to contact the following museums/art galleries:

Goya: *El Tres de Mayo de 1808 en Madrid*: Museo del Prado, Madrid, Spain
Manet: *L'Enfant des Cerises*: Museu Calouste Gulbenkian, Avenida de Berna, 1093 Lisboa Codex, Portugal
Jan van Eyck: *The Arnolfini Marriage*: The National Gallery, Trafalgar Square, London WC2 5DN, UK

Note, however, that these paintings serve here just as models for a technique and many other paintings work just as well.

2 Decide exactly how to exploit the painting. This will depend on several factors – the number of main characters in the painting, how emotionally charged the painting is and what else is in the painting.

A Goya: *El Tres de Mayo de 1808 en Madrid*
You can use this painting in the context of work on the topic of war or conflict.

Procedure

1 Give out one postcard of this painting to each pair or three, according to the number of students and number of cards you have. Alternatively, show a poster or project a slide of the painting.

Fig. 10

2 Ask each pair/three to write fifteen questions they would like to ask the man in the white shirt who is about to be shot. Insist they write at least fifteen, but allow for some only thinking of ten to twelve.

3 Choose a student to take the role of the victim. In general (though not always) I find that it is better to choose a girl/woman to take the role – girls/women tend to be better at identifying with him. Put a chair at the front of the class and ask the 'victim' to come and sit on it.

4 Ask the rest of the class to ask the 'victim' their questions, which the 'victim' should try to answer.

NOTE

This is a highly-charged painting with less scope for a wide range of questions than a lot of paintings. The few questions tend to focus on the victim's feelings, his belief or not in God or an after-life, the other people in the painting that have been shot or are about to be shot, the executioners, their attitude towards the victim and his attitude towards them. The questions and answers bring home in a very direct way the profoundly human quality of the painting.

Fig. 11

B Manet: *L'Enfant des Cerises*
You can use this painting in the context of the topic of people, especially children.

Procedure

As with **A**, but increase the number of questions to twenty (allowing for some students only writing fifteen), as the boy is a very inspiring character.

NOTE

This painting is remarkable for the way it makes the viewer, whether male or female, identify with the boy. There are a number of similar paintings by Vermeer and his Dutch contemporaries centred on a single figure. The presence of objects portrayed in detail in these pictures often leads the students to ask curious and penetrating questions.

C Jan van Eyck: *The Arnolfini Marriage*

You can use this painting in the context of people, relationships, social class and clothing. The presence of two people and a dog allows for an importantly different variation in procedure.

Fig. 12

Procedure

1 Divide the class into groups of three. Give each group at least one copy of the painting or show a poster or project a slide of it so that everyone can see it.

2 Tell your students to take a fresh sheet of paper. Ask one student (A) in each group to write five questions to ask the man, ask another (B) to write five to ask the woman and ask the third (C) to write five to ask the dog. Ask them to write the character (man, woman or dog) at the head of their sheet.

3 When they have each written their five questions, ask them to pass their sheet clockwise round the group. According to the character (man, woman or dog) at the head of the sheet, each student must add five new questions to ask the character.

4 When they have each written their five questions, ask them once more to pass their sheet clockwise round the group. Again, according to the character named at the head of the sheet, they add five more questions.

5 When they have finished their questions, they keep the sheet they have just been working on. They remain in their groups of three. The student with the fifteen questions for the man asks the student who wrote the first five of them (Student A) to answer them all. Student A does so. Repeat this process with the questions for the woman and the dog.

On pages 73–5 are three sets of questions that one upper intermediate group came up with while doing this activity. The corrections were made soon after collecting the sets of questions in.

NOTE
I have rarely known students get so hysterical with laughter as with Step 5 using this painting.

ACKNOWLEDGEMENTS
My choice of paintings owes a good deal to John Berger's BBC television series 'Ways of seeing', also available in book form (Berger 1972). His emphasis on getting people to respond to paintings in their own way has helped me a lot in coming to this activity and Activity 3.5 *Painting into poem*. Cynthia Beresford introduced me to the idea of writing questions and answering in role at a seminar at the British Council, Lisbon in September 1986.

The Man

① Are you dead?
② Are you a priest?
③ Why are you wearing a hat indoors? inside ✓✓
④ Why are you so slim?
⑤ Don't you like ~~to go~~ to the beach?
   going

- How much did it cost ~~you~~, ~~the~~ picture? to have your done

- How did you manage to ~~keep~~ the dog in that position?

- How old are you?

- Do you have any other children?

- What is ~~waiting~~ written on the ~~x~~ wall?

→ Why do you have a ring on ~~the~~ your right hand?

→ How can you ~~use~~ wear such an hat ~~so~~ awful?

→ Why do you have ~~you~~ ~~the~~ your right hand in that position?

→ Did you know that you are in a picture reflected in the mirror and would you like to see it?

→ Aren't you afraid that the chandelier will fall and kill you?

Fig. 13

Woman

Where are you looking at *in* the ~~photograph~~ *Picture*?

Is he the father of the child?

Are you at your home?

How long have you been pregnant?

How long ~~had~~ *did* you *have* to stay in that position
so that the *a.* pinter could do this picture?

→ Why do you have your right hand turned upwards?

→ Which of the two pairs of shoes ~~are~~ *is* yours?

→ Why don't you have a marriage ring?

→ Why don't you put the lamps missing in the chandelier?

→ Why is your room so untidy?

- Who is your hairdresser?
- Do you feel well under those heavy clothes?
- Are you sad?
- Who is the baby's father?
- Why are you holding your dress?

Fig. 13 (continued)

Dog

- Why are you so still and in that position?
- Why is your hair so colned? = combed?
- Are you a male or a female?
- What (you) are feeling beyond those black eyes?
- Why don't you run from such a dark room?

- What's your name?
- Are you real?
- What are you thinking about, food?
- Who are those people? Your owners?
- Do you like cats?

- where are you looking at?

- How old are you?

- Have you any puppies?

- How did they manage to keep you in that position?

- Are they your owners?

Fig. 13 (continued)

3.5

FOCUS
Stimulating the
imagination;
Writing poetry

MATERIALS
Poster/slide/
postcards of (a)
painting(s);
Slide projector
(optional)

TIME
20–40 minutes

PAINTING INTO POEM

In this activity you can have all your students working on the same painting or pairs working on several different ones. The paintings need to include people doing things of some kind. To illustrate, I shall use Turner's painting, *The Shipwreck of the Minotaur*. You could also try paintings by Lowry, the Breughels and Anton Pieck, among others.

Procedure

1 Divide the class into pairs. Either project a painting with slide and projector or distribute postcard reproductions, one per pair, or display a poster.
2 Ask each pair to look at the slide or the poster or their postcard and according to what they see in the painting write down twelve adjectives, eight nouns and six verbs ending in *-ing*.
3 Tell the pairs that they are to write a poem using all of the words they have written down and no others except articles, possessives, prepositions, *and*, *or*, *but*, *yes* and *no*. I occasionally allow other words but never extra nouns, adjectives or verbs of any kind – be as firm as possible. They may only use each word once, unless it is for deliberate rhetorical repetition. You will find that they write the first few lines quite quickly and easily, but it is the last few that challenge the imagination, and that is the whole point of the activity.

Fig. 14

To give you an idea of what to expect, here are the words chosen by two of my students, followed by the poem they wrote from them (all uncorrected; note, for example that *darkness* should have been in the noun column). It is a typical, not exceptional, piece of work.

Adjectives	*Nouns*	*Verbs*
darkness	shipwreck	rowing
lonely	ocean	praying
furious	uncertainty	sinking
bloody	batle	fighting
scared	men	suffering
miserable	despair	frightening
deadly	death	
stormy	nature	
anguish		
desperate		
powefull		
helpless		

Shipwreck
In the powefull furious ocean,
desperate men rowing,
fighting against death.
Helpless and lonely,
Miserable behind the frightening Nature . . .
Praying . . .

Sinking their anguish,
in darkness uncertainty,
scared to death.
Suffering in despair,
in a bloody deadly batle . . .
Praying . . .
   Maria João and Rita

NOTES

a This activity illustrates the saying 'Necessity is the mother of invention'. It is the extreme restrictiveness of this procedure that makes it so effective.

b You can obtain postcards/slides of Turner's *The Shipwreck of the Minotaur* from the Museu Calouste Gulbenkian, Avenida de Berna, 1093 Lisboa Codex, Portugal, but remember there are many other paintings that can be used in this way which may be available to you more easily.

ACKNOWLEDGEMENTS
The inspiration behind this activity is Anita Straker's computer program 'Wordplay'. I have used a similar procedure with a different type of input in the activity 'A walk through the seasons' in *The Standby Book* (Lindstromberg, forthcoming).

3.6

FOCUS
Visualising a
scene through
music

MATERIALS
Cassette recorder
and cassette;
4 half-class sets of
the Handouts;
A recording of
Debussy's *Prélude
à l'après-midi d'un
faune*

TIME
50–60 minutes

MUSICAL DESCRIPTION

There are many ways of exploiting music for its power to suggest images. In this activity, which I use from mid-intermediate level upwards, we look at how it can suggest a single image and thus description, while in the next one, Activity 3.7 *Musical narrative*, we will concentrate on music that suggests a series of images and thus a narrative.

Preparation

You need multiple copies of the four Handouts 1A and 1B, 2A and 2B on pages 80–1. Make enough copies of each set for half your class.

Procedure

1 Tell your class that you are going to divide them into two halves (A and B) and each half will be doing different tasks. Divide the class. Within each half put them into pairs. Give out instructions 1A to the pairs in the A half and 1B to the pairs in the B half. Tell them they have fifteen minutes to carry out their instructions. (If they need a little longer, give an extra five minutes, but not more.)

2 Put the pairs from the A half into groups of six or eight and do the same with the B half. Ask the pairs to compare their notes with the others in their group and to add anything they think is important to their own notes. Don't spend more than ten minutes on this.

3 Tell your students you are going to play them a piece of music and that once again you are going to give different instructions to the two halves of the class. Give out instructions 2A to the A half and 2B to the B half. Tell them to follow the instructions and that it is important that they work individually without talking to one another or looking at what others are writing.

4 Play Debussy's *Prélude à l'après-midi d'un faune*. When the music has finished, give your students enough time to go on writing till they have written all they want to.

5 Ask them to return to the groups of six or eight formed in Step 2 above and to tell one another what they wrote.

6 Regroup the class into groups of four, each group consisting of a pair from the A half and a pair from the B half. Ask them to tell the pair from the other group what they have been doing, what they heard in the music and what others heard.

NOTES

a Here are some uncorrected examples of what some intermediate students have heard:

Animals

● 'The music reminds me of a rabbit. The kind that lives in forests, looking for food, cautiously because of his natural enemys like the fox. With the idea of a rabbit comes freedom, danger, survival.'

● 'A sawn [*swan*]. It – for me, it is more like a female character; so, a "she" – is fragile and, at this moment, very sad. It slowly dances, expressing is deep feelings. It is very kind and gracious, and its mouvements are quick and strong, yet calm and docile. It embraces the music and lets itself being taken away by the melody. It is divided inside. By the strong and courageous melody and the deep instability of the violins.'

Time of day

● 'I think is morning. At least, that's the way it may me think. The music it's very calm but simultaneously "gives" us the idea that something is waking up or growing – the music really remember me those films, we see the little birds and animals in the forests in the morning. This music started very easily an ten became in a progressive way more lively, however, without rush. That's exactly the way I feel in the morning: with energy but too lazzy to make a movement.'

I find a number of tendencies in student responses. Firstly, of the animals, they often hear rabbits, swans and squirrels. Secondly, most people hear dawn and sunrise or morning rather than some other time of day. Many students hear animals though they are listening for a time of day, while a few that are listening for animals also imagine them at a certain time of day.

Debussy was describing a 'faun', a minor classical deity that protects shepherds, in the afternoon, in accordance with Mallarmé's poem of the same name, which inspired it.

b You will find a number of music-based activities focusing on description in *Musical Openings* (Cranmer and Laroy 1992), especially in Chapters five and six.

HANDOUT 1A FOR ACTIVITY 3.6

With a partner, write down the names of any animals you can think of (including birds, fishes, insects, etc.). Describe the way they move and the kind of noise they make.

....

....

....

....

....

....

....

....

....

....

....

Cranmer *Motivating High Level Learners*
© Addison Wesley Longman Limited 1996   Photocopiable

✂ ---

HANDOUT 1B FOR ACTIVITY 3.6

With a partner, write down words and phrases you associate with these times of day:

dawn and sunrise: ....

....

morning: ....

....

midday: ....

....

afternoon: ....

....

sunset and dusk: ....

....

evening: ....

....

night: ....

....

Cranmer *Motivating High Level Learners*
© Addison Wesley Longman Limited 1996   Photocopiable

HANDOUT 2A FOR ACTIVITY 3.6

The piece of music you are going to listen to describes an animal. What kind of animal do you think it is? What do you hear it doing? Write brief notes as you listen.

....

....

....

....

....

....

....

....

....

....

....

Cranmer *Motivating High Level Learners*
© Addison Wesley Longman Limited 1996   **Photocopiable**

HANDOUT 2B FOR ACTIVITY 3.6

The piece of music you are going to listen to describes a time of day. What time of day do you think it is? What do you hear in the music that gives you that impression? Write brief notes as you listen.

....

....

....

....

....

....

....

....

....

....

....

....

....

Cranmer *Motivating High Level Learners*
© Addison Wesley Longman Limited 1996   **Photocopiable**

3.7

FOCUS
Visualising a story
through music;
Vocabulary
relating to battles

MATERIALS
Cassette player
and cassette of
music describing
a battle

TIME
30–50 minutes

MUSICAL NARRATIVE

This activity exploits music's power to evoke a series of images and thus to imply a narrative. In this instance the narrative describes a battle and would therefore fit in well with the topic 'war' or 'conflict' as well as work on narrative building. Of the pieces I have used Walton's 'Charge and battle' from the *Henry V Suite* works best.

If you cannot obtain the Walton, you could try Beethoven's *'Battle Symphony'*, Op. 91, 'Mars' from Holst's *The Planets* (there is a recording of the finale of this in the cassette that accompanies Activity 4.5 of *Musical Openings* [Cranmer and Laroy 1992]), or shorter battles such as the battle scene from Richard Strauss's *Ein Heldenleben* or Variation II from his *Don Quixote* (in which Don Quixote takes on a flock of sheep!).

Procedure

1 Divide the class into three groups. Subdivide each group into pairs or threes. Tell your students you would like to work with them on vocabulary that has to do with land battles. Ask one group to write down the names of weapons, one to write down names of types of people involved in battles, one to write down verbs to do with battles. Remind them to think about different periods. Give a time limit of ten minutes.

2 Draw three columns on the board and head them *weapons, people* and *actions*. Ask the groups to tell you the words in their lists and write them on the board. Make sure that they include weapons of all periods (including *sword, spear, dagger, bow and arrow*), a good range of people (*cavalry, archers,* as well as *infantry* and *artillery*) and a good range of actions (including *charge, attack, defend*). Also make sure your students know the use of the definite article + adjective expressions *the dead, the wounded.*

3 Tell the class you are going to play them a piece of music describing a battle. Ask them as they listen, to imagine the battle and write a description of the battle they hear. Suggest that it is best as they listen to decide roughly when and between whom the battle took place.

4 Play the music.

5 Give your students up to ten minutes additional time to finish what they are writing. Put them into groups of five or six and tell them to pass their descriptions round the group for one another to read. Then ask them to pair up with another student from a different group. Tell them to compare the similarities and differences between the ways their respective groups heard the battle.

NOTES

a Listening to the Walton, students tend to hear battles set in the 18th or 19th centuries rather than in the Middle Ages. One student of mine heard it as a sea battle between two galleys set in Roman times. Here are two uncorrected battle texts written by students, one in class, exactly as described above, the other (a poem) was done at home just after we had done this activity, written by a student who had systematically done no homework till then (for a term and a half) – this activity marked the turning point in his attitude towards all we were doing in class and towards his colleagues and me.

The American Civil War: the infantry is coming forward with drummer in front. The general keeps giving orders as they approach the enemy.
Suddenly, this image is replaced by a battlefield in the middle ages. There are arrows flying, wounded men falling from their horses, and the sound of the armors as they hit the ground. The air is filled with moans, screams and blood.
The battle ends, the smell of gunpowder wafts through the air and the field is coverd with wounded and dead corpses.
   Paulo

Poem
The plain was silent
And everything was assleep
Gods and Men lived
In harmony and peace.
Suddenly, the canons roar
The bombs fell
The guns shot and
the field that once was quiet
Now became a kingdom
Of pain and horror.
The smell of death is in the air
And the innocent child
Called Peace
Dies by the trembling hands
Of the surprised boys
Transformed into men.
While the Gods, threatned
By this show of misery,
Run away to the Eden
Closing its door
To the helpless humanity
   Luís

b For a variety of other ways of exploiting the narrative quality of music, see Chapter four of *Musical Openings* (Cranmer and Laroy 1992).

3.8

FOCUS
Ten principles of
creativity

MATERIALS
Photocopies of
the Handout 'Ten
principles of
creativity'
(optional)

TIME
30 minutes

'PIGS MIGHT FLY'

If your students think they have no imagination, prove them wrong
with this activity. It introduces ten principles of creativity, illustrates
them and applies them to ghost stories.

Preparation

Make copies of the Handout on page 87, one for each student. If you
don't have copying facilities you will have to write the handout onto
the board for your students to copy into their notebooks, but it
wastes a lot of time and distracts the class from what you are
explaining.

Procedure

1 Draw a large cloud on the left-hand side of the board. Ask your
  students to copy it. Then ask them, working alone, to write in
  their cloud any characteristics of ghosts they can think of and
  anything associated with ghosts. If they are uncertain what kind
  of things to put, suggest that these may be: adjectives, e.g. *transparent, frightening*; nouns, e.g. *chains, cemeteries*; or verbs, e.g.
  groan, haunt. Set a time limit of two minutes and be strict about it.

2 After the two minutes are up, divide the class into pairs and get
  them to compare the ghost characteristics/associations with their
  partner. They can add any of their partner's thoughts to their own
  cloud.

3 Tell the class that you will return to the clouds later, but now you
  want them to put their pens down and close their books, so that
  they can give you full attention. Tell them that you want to give
  them a short talk about principles of creativity – ways of being
  imaginative when they can't think of anything. You will be describing ten principles and then working with the class to apply them
  to composition writing. Explain that most of the principles are
  taken from the visual arts.

4 Talk your students through the Handout on page 87 but don't give
  it out yet. For each principle, simply write the number and the
  principle on the right-hand side of the board. Then give them an
  example or two to illustrate each principle.

5 Give out copies of the Handout, one to each student.

6 Ask them to go back to their ghost clouds. Ask them what they
  wrote and add them to your cloud on the board. Probably it will
  look something like this:

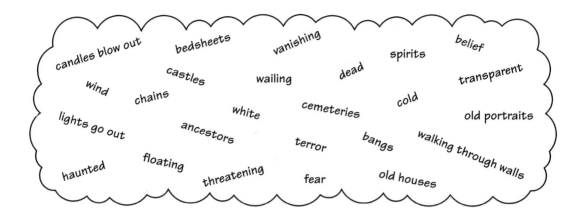

candles blow out   bedsheets   vanishing   spirits   belief

wind   castles   wailing   dead   transparent

chains   white   cemeteries   cold

lights go out   ancestors   old portraits

haunted   floating   terror   bangs   walking through walls

threatening   fear   old houses

7 Now talk your students through how you could apply the ten creative principles to the characteristics of ghosts to see what original ghost stories you can come up with.

Principle one – Change the dimension
We tend to think of ghosts as being human-sized. Suppose we had a giant ghost or a mini-ghost, or a combination of sizes, such as a daddy ghost, a mummy ghost and some baby ghosts.

Principle two – Change the colour
In the characteristics we saw that ghosts are normally white or transparent. Why not have one that is orange and goes bright green when it blushes?

Principle three – Change the material
Ghosts are supposed either to have no substance or to be like bedsheets. But a ghost could be made of stone or liquid.

Principle four – Change the place
You usually find ghosts in castles, cemeteries and old houses, but why not in the sitting room or kitchen of a modern flat? Or maybe the ghost has come from another planet or star, or a human ghost is on another planet or star.

Principle five – Change the time (anachronism)
Ghosts are usually linked to the past, the dead. Suppose we had a ghost of someone from the future. Or you could set the story in the future and you are the ghost.

Principle six – Change the purpose
We normally think of ghosts as terrifying and threatening. They could also be warm, friendly and welcoming, helping us to do the washing up and the ironing.

Principle seven – Change the velocity or type of movement
You could have an ultra-high-speed ghost that goes zooming around, or one that swims instead of flying.

Principle eight – Multiply
Rather than write a story about one ghost, write about a whole city haunted by thousands of ghosts.

Principle nine – Reverse, e.g. roles
Instead of the ghost haunting humans, humans could haunt a ghost.

Principle ten – Animate or personify
Instead of the ghost being of an ex-human it could be of an ex-animal. Combined with the principle of reversing you could create an inanimate ghost, for example a ghost chair that vanishes just as you are about to sit on it.

8 With these ideas you will have fired their enthusiasm, so do not hesitate to set this composition task for homework: 'Write an original ghost story, about 300 words long'. If you wish, you can hold a competition for the most original ghost story. Alternatively, as a more co-operative venture, you could suggest that the class puts together a collection of 'Ghost stories with a difference'.

ACKNOWLEDGEMENTS
The ten creative principles are derived from those put forward by Bruno Munari in *Fantasia* (Munari 1987). Some of the examples given above are also his. I first described their application to composition writing in an article 'Teaching more advanced learners' (Cranmer 1990/91).

HANDOUT FOR ACTIVITY 3.8

Ten principles of creativity and examples of each

Principle one – Change the dimension

The Belgian Surrealist painter Magritte produced a painting with a comb, glass, match, shaving brush and bar of soap inside a room, but each of these was proportionately much bigger than the bed and the wardrobe in the same room. Horror films often use this principle, e.g. *King Kong*, films with giant spiders or other animals.

Principle two – Change the colour

Some punks dye their hair bright green or purple or some other colour that is not a natural hair colour.

Principle three – Change the material

Salvador Dali, the famous Spanish Surrealist painter, did a painting called *The persistence of memory* which has watches made of rubber instead of metal and glass. Instead of being rigid, they flop.

Principle four – Change the place

Imagine London with canals instead of streets or Venice with streets instead of canals.

Principle five – Change the time (anachronism)

Imagine a prehistoric man listening to a wind-up gramophone or Napoleon using a computer.

Principle six – Change the purpose

Some people use empty bottles as candle-holders or hang objects on the wall for decoration.

Principle seven – Change the velocity or type of movement

Aesop wrote the fable of the hare and the tortoise, but imagine a tortoise that could really run faster than a hare. Imagine a flying pig or crocodile.

Principle eight – Multiply

Indian gods and goddesses are often depicted with many arms, heads etc.

Principle nine – Reverse, e.g. roles

Imagine birds or animals looking at humans in a cage, resting a saucer on a cup and drinking from the saucer.

Principle ten – Animate or personify

Snowmen that come to life, Gerard Hoffnung's animations of musical instruments.

Cranmer *Motivating High Level Learners*
© Addison Wesley Longman Limited 1996 Photocopiable

3.9

FOCUS
Extending the use
of the ten creative
principles

MATERIALS
None

TIME
15 minutes each
on two occasions

CREATIVE PRINCIPLES APPLIED

This activity assumes you have already done the previous Activity 3.8 *'Pigs might fly'*. Do Steps 1 to 5 in one lesson and 6 to 7 in another, a week or two later.

Procedure

1 Refer your students to the ten creative principles you worked on in Activity 3.8. Ask them to reread the handout you distributed in Step 5.

2 According to most people ghosts are a figment of human fantasy. Explain to your students that for this reason ghosts lend themselves to imaginative treatment. The ten creative principles are not always so simple to apply with other subjects and indeed in some cases you have to use other ways of generating ideas. (See Activity 4.5 *The random object*.) Here we will look at two composition types – narrative and discursive – and apply the ten principles to them.

3 Give the class a narrative title, e.g. 'The picnic'. On the left-hand side of the board, list the ten creative principles and tell them to copy these down. Ask your students to work individually and see how they might apply the ten principles to the title. Tell them that they won't be able to think of ideas for all principles, but that in order to write an imaginative composition they don't need very many. Set a time limit of two minutes and no more. (You must stick rigidly to the time limit, so that they get used to the idea that this is something that can be done very quickly.)

4 When the two minutes are up, ask the class to put their pens down. Be very insistent on this. Ask them what ideas they have come up with. Just to give you an idea of some of the possibilities, these are the ideas I had when I gave myself two minutes:

1 Dimension: How many people were present?
2 Colour: Were there foods of different colours or people/cuisines of different races/nations?
3 Material: –
4 Place: Where? Indoors, or in town, for a change?
5 Time: When? A winter's evening, for a change?
6 Purpose: –
7 Velocity/movement: –
8 Multiplication: Lots of people having picnics at the same time in the same place?
9 Reversal: Many picnics are arranged by adults for children, why not children arranging one for adults?
10 Personification/animation: –

As you will see, I had no ideas for principles 3, 6, 7 and 10. This doesn't matter, as there are more than enough ideas here for a picnic with a difference.

5 Give your students another narrative title, e.g. 'A day when every-thing went wrong', and once again give them a time limit of two minutes to note down any ideas, using the ten creative principles. After the two minutes are up, tell them to write a composition for homework taking one of the titles they have been working on and using some of the collective ideas for 'The Picnic' or their own ideas for 'A day when everything went wrong'.

6 In a later lesson, a week or two later, repeat the same process as above (Steps 3 to 5) but with discursive titles. Write the title on the board, e.g. 'Discuss the statement "A woman's place is in the home"'. Write the ten creative principles on the left of the board and give your students three minutes (as it takes a little longer than with narratives) to jot down ideas related to the subject. After the three minutes are up, ask the class for their ideas. These were my ideas when I gave myself three minutes:

1 Dimension: How widespread a view is this?
2 Colour: (politics) Is this attitude more typical of conservatives, liberals, socialists? (culture) Is this attitude more typical of some cultures than others?
3 Material: –
4 Place: Where else might a woman's place be?
5 Time: Has this attitude always prevailed? Is it changing nowadays?
6 Purpose: –
7 Velocity/movement: –
8 Multiplication: Does this apply to other members of the household than the wife/mother?
9 Reversal: Househusbands
10 Personification/animation: Machines that do what women used to do – How far does this alter women's position?

Once again you will notice that not all the principles generated ideas, but there are plenty here for a more imaginative composi-tion.

7 Give your students another discursive title, e.g. 'Discuss the state-ment "Money is the root of all evil"', and once again give them a time limit of three minutes to note down any ideas, using the ten creative principles. After the time is up, tell them to write a com-position for homework taking one of the discursive titles they have been working on and using some of the collective ideas for 'A woman's place is in the home' or their own ideas for 'Money is the root of all evil'.

CHAPTER 4

Thinking

'Piglet said, "How shall we do it?" and Pooh said, "that's just it.
How?" And they sat down together to think it out.'*
   A. A. Milne

This chapter looks at thinking in relation to composition writing and
problem solving.

4.1

FOCUS
Raising student
awareness of the
stages they
should go through
when they write a
composition

MATERIALS
None

TIME
20–40 minutes

COMPOSITION STAGES

Do this activity early in a course, if possible before setting a first
composition.

Procedure

1 Ask your students to identify and discuss the stages they go
through in producing a composition. Allow two to three minutes
and then ask for feedback. With a bit of luck they will identify at
least three stages: planning, writing and checking. Put it to them
that planning involves two related but separate notions: generating ideas and organising them.
2 On the board draw this flow chart:

GENERATE IDEAS
ORGANISE IDEAS
WRITE
CHECK AND EDIT

Put it to the students that two of these stages are free stages
while the other two involve rigorous control. Ask them which are
which. Generating ideas should be free, then controlled through
organising. Writing should be free, then controlled by checking
and editing.
3 The notion that the writing stage should be a free one may meet
strong opposition from students who are used to doing everything (thinking, organising, writing, checking and editing) all at
the same time. Students whose general manner is highly controlled may also find it very hard to cope with this notion. In

*Piglet and Pooh are characters in the children's books *Winnie-the-Pooh* and *The House at
Pooh Corner.*

either case they may be rather defensive in their way of doing things. Coax this out into the open and deal with it in a class discussion. Be prepared to counter objections like these:

'I don't need to plan.'
'Planning reduces my spontaneity.'
'I don't find in reality I have time to plan.'
'I don't find I have time to check and edit.'

Invite counter-arguments from the class to defuse these and any other objections that are raised, helping if necessary. Here are some counter-arguments:

a You may not need to plan, but planning usually results in a composition with richer content and clearer organisation.
b Plans need not be followed rigidly, but should act as a point of departure, to be used as a servant, not obeyed as a master.
c Many people are afraid of running out of time because of planning, but curiously this point is never raised by those who *do* plan.
d In an exam, by planning you quickly discover whether or not you can answer a question or not. If you find you can't, you can shift rapidly to another question. If you only write without planning, you waste a lot more time before you discover you don't have enough to say.
e If you plan *what* you are going to say and the order to say it in before writing, you can concentrate on the language to say it with while writing.
f Having time to check is simply a question of allocating time for it before-hand and keeping roughly to your timing.

4 Either go directly on to Activity 4.2 or 4.3 or, alternatively, give the class two composition titles, a narrative and an expository/argumentative one, for example:

a Write a story involving a piece of cheese, a fire escape, and a retired doctor.
b In what ways are you optimistic and/or pessimistic about the future of the world?

The length of each composition should be about 250 words. Tell them that you want them to do one in class and the other for homework – it doesn't matter which they do where. Stress the importance of following the stages you have been discussing, and insist they spend at least ten minutes planning (generating and organising ideas) before they start writing. Control and supervise them rigorously on this. Note, however, that this is not an exam, so you should help them with any difficulties they have. For the same reason, a time limit is not appropriate for the writing stage. If, for practical reasons (the length of the lesson or the need to do other things in the same lesson), you need to cut them short, do so and let them complete their first compositions at home to deliver to you next lesson without fail. When they have finished writing or in the next lesson, as appropriate, give ten minutes for them to check and edit their compositions before handing them in to you. Ask them to follow this whole procedure for the second composition, but in their own time at home. Set a deadline for handing it in.

4.2

FOCUS
Generating and organising ideas for a composition

MATERIALS
A blank sheet of paper

TIME
40–60 minutes

THE BRAINSTORM PLAN

Procedure

1 Initiate a discussion with your class on how easy they find it to think of ideas for compositions and how they organise ideas once they've got them. After a brief discussion tell them you are going to work with them on a simple technique to use when they have a series of ideas but are unsure how to connect them and about what order to present them in, i.e. the problem is not so much the ideas as the organisation.

2 Ask your students to take a piece of paper and pencil (or pen). Tell them to turn the paper to landscape position, i.e. with the long side at the top and bottom, and to draw lines randomly in different positions on the page. Demonstrate it yourself on the board.

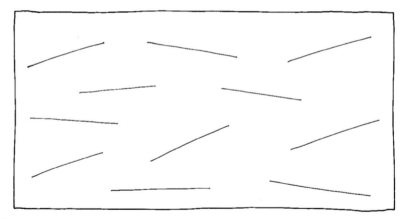

Fig. 15

3 Give them a title, for example 'The problems of adolescence/being elderly/being a parent/being a prime minister'. Get them to work individually and write down any ideas they have on the title, spreading them on the random lines all over the page. When your students have run out of ideas, put them into groups of three or four to share and discuss their ideas. One of my students, Sara, recently made this plan on the problems of adolescence (uncorrected):

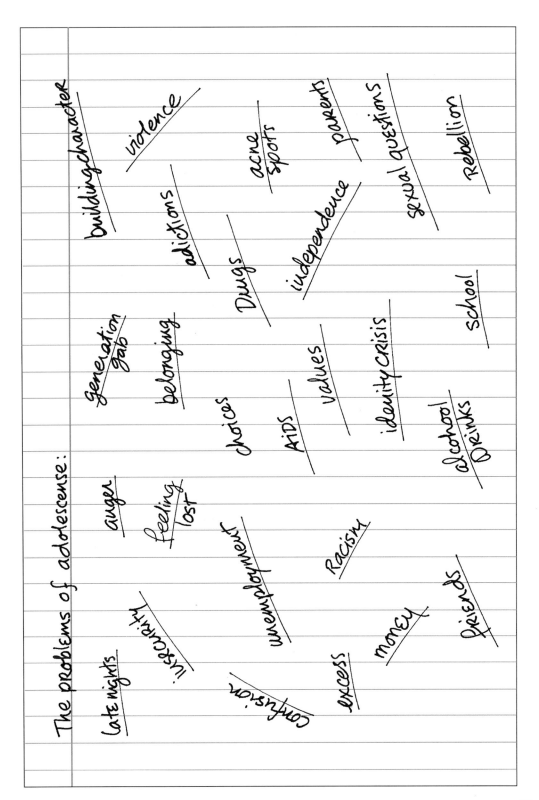

The problems of adolescence:

building character
violence
acne spots
parents
sexual questions
Rebellion
adictions
Drugs
independence
school
generation gap
belonging
choices
AIDS
values
identity crisis
alcohol Drinks
anger
feeling lost
unemployment
Racism
money
friends
late nights
insecurity
confusion
excess

Fig. 16

93

4 Ask the class for their ideas and write them spread randomly on the board. When you have done this, ask them what effect sharing and discussing their ideas had. They should find that this has the effect of generating more ideas than they had at first.

5 Ask the class what connections they see between the various ideas on the board. Indicate the connections they mention by drawing a line between the ideas in question to form groups of ideas. (It is important, as far as possible, to make sure that the lines don't cross. If they do cross, the plan is inclined to become confusing. You can also increase the clarity by connecting the groups of ideas in different colours.) Decide if there are any ideas you want to discard. If so, put a line through them. Now ask the groups of three or four, as in Step 3, to decide on a possible order to present both the groups of ideas and the separate ideas within each group. Students tend to want to do this in one of two ways: either by taking the plan, numbering the idea groups and giving letters to the ideas within each group, or by taking a separate sheet and copying the idea groups, usually linearly, into the order they want to use when they present the ideas. There are always several possible orders.

6 Ask the groups about the order they decided on. Unless there are very clear preferences, try to avoid arguments about right and wrong orders, emphasising that there may be many different possibilities.

7 Set the title you have chosen as a composition for homework and ask the students to incorporate the groups of ideas in it.

NOTE

The insistence on paper in landscape position and drawing the random lines is important. We tend to get into the habit of thinking linearly down a page in 'portrait' position, i.e. with the short side along top and bottom. When we are thinking about things that are not intrinsically linear, this is singularly unhelpful. This exercise is aimed among other things at breaking the tyranny of lines.

THE MIND MAP PLAN

Do this activity soon after Activity 4.2 *The brainstorm plan*.

Preparation

Choose a topic that puts forward views but not one with two sharply divided sides (i.e. not a 'for and against' or 'advantages and disadvantages' type). By way of example, we will take the title: 'What I consider important in life'.

Procedure

1 Tell your class that you are going to introduce them to a type of essay plan similar to the brainstorm plan. Explain that this type is most useful for discursive compositions where you have a reasonably clear idea of the main points you want to make, but need to work out the details and the order of presentation.
2 Write the title in the middle of the board. Ask your students to take a sheet of paper. Ask them to turn it round sideways so that the long side is at the top and bottom. This means that the lines of lined paper do not operate, which reduces the temptation to think and plan linearly. Tell them to write the title in the middle.
3 Ask them what main areas they might want to write about in a composition with this title. Write them on the board, linked to the title with a line. The board might look something like this:

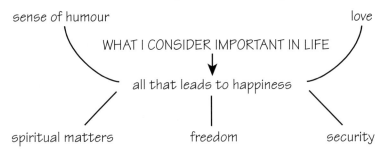

Fig. 17

4 Divide the class into pairs. Ask the pairs to work on this 'mind map' skeleton and do two things: expand each main area with further points and decide the order to present the areas in.

Tell them to write the additional points near the main area each relates to and to join it with a line. As with the brainstorm plan, suggest they number and letter the ideas to indicate the order of presentation. Allow about fifteen minutes for this.
5 Join the pairs together to make groups of four and compare ideas and orders of presentation.
6 In pairs again, get them to decide on a brief introduction and conclusion.
7 Set the title you have chosen as a composition for homework.

4.3

FOCUS
Generating and organising ideas for a composition

MATERIALS
A blank sheet of paper

TIME
30–45 minutes

NOTES

a By way of example, this is the mind map I wrote on one occasion when I tackled this composition under timed conditions while my students did the same composition. (My original plan and composition were in Portuguese.)

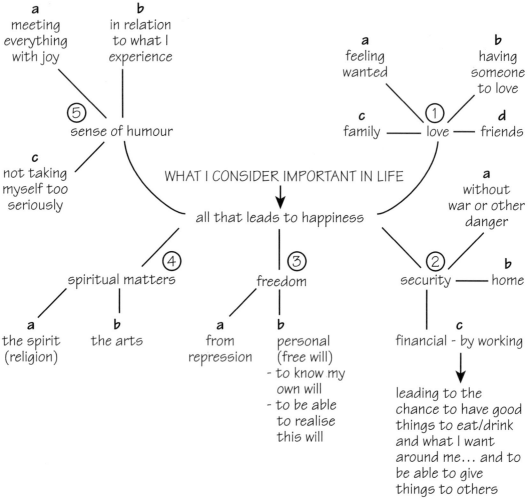

Fig. 18

b Mind map plans are extremely versatile once you get used to using them and can be adapted without great difficulty to all discursive composition types and used equally as a basis for oral presentations as well as for compositions.

c There are some descriptive topics where mind map plans come in useful but because of the difficulty in organising pure descriptions I generally prefer to use a brainstorm plan. I find that narratives, because time acts as the main organising factor, rarely benefit from the use of mind map plans.

ACKNOWLEDGEMENTS
Mind maps were invented by Tony Buzan and he describes them in detail in *Use Your Head* (Buzan 1974). I first described their use in foreign language teaching in the articles 'Notes, summaries and compositions' (Cranmer 1985).

THE MIND MAP SUMMARY

4.4

FOCUS
Summary writing using mind map plans

Summary writing, such as that required by the University of Cambridge Certificate of Proficiency in English, often causes students difficulty. I have found this rather different way of going about summary writing consistently effective with my students.

MATERIALS
Photocopies of the text by
R. K. Narayan;
Photocopies of the Worksheet (see Variations)

Preparation

Make multiple copies, one for each student, of the text by the Indian writer R. K. Narayan on page 102–3.

TIME
40–60 minutes

Procedure

1 Hand out copies of the text, one to each student.
2 Instruct your students to underline any vocabulary they do not understand. When they have done so, go through it with them, eliciting explanations as far as possible from the class.
3 Tell them that you are going to work with them on summary writing and will show them a simple method of doing this.
4 Tell your students to suppose, as in a Proficiency Examination, that they have been set the task 'In a paragraph of 70–90 words, summarise the symptoms of old age and their consequences, according to the writer'. Ask them to identify what precisely the task asks them to summarise: the *symptoms* of old age and their *consequences*. Write this in the middle of the board and draw a box around it (fig. 19).

THE SYMPTOMS OF OLD AGE
AND THEIR CONSEQUENCES

Fig. 19

5 Put your students into pairs and ask them to decide on the symptoms that the text describes. When they are ready, ask them what they found and write them on the board, radiating from the central box. My students generally recognise five: growing deaf, absent-mindedness, forgetfulness, falling, the body demands constant attention. Any others, after discussion, we have always agreed were consequences. The board should now look something like fig. 20:

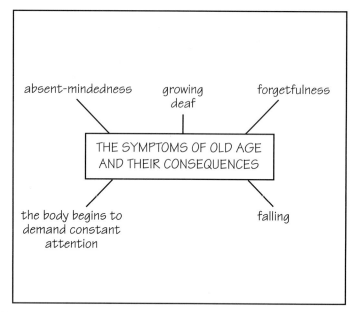

Fig. 20

6 Having established the symptoms, now ask your students, once again in pairs, to note down the consequences, according to the text. As before, when they are ready, ask them what they found and add them to the diagram on the board, radiating from the appropriate symptom. My students generally identify the following: you don't hear the phone ringing (growing deaf), misplacing things (absent-mindedness), you can't remember names and faces (forgetfulness), you have to 'mend your conduct' = change your behaviour (falling), travel becomes impossible (falling), an overwhelming medical schedule (the body begins to demand constant attention), dependence (general). The board should now look something like fig. 21:

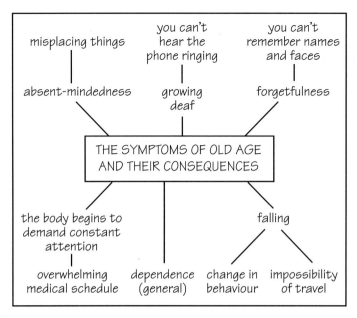

Fig. 21

7 Ask your students, again in pairs, to draw connections between related points and decide on the best order to present them in the summary. When they have decided, ask for suggestions. Generally speaking, there is agreement that physical symptoms and their consequences should be separated from mental ones, but that within that the order is not important. Come to an agreement with the class as to a possible order and number the points on the board accordingly.

8 Remind your students of useful summary beginnings and endings, together with connectors of enumeration and addition. I suggest the following:

Beginnings
The writer mentions (number) (items) (in this case 'five symptoms')
According to the writer there are (number) (items)

Endings
In general,
To conclude,

Connectors of enumeration
Firstly,
Secondly,
Lastly,
(with a tight word limit *In the first place*, etc. is very wasteful)

Connectors of addition
Furthermore,
In addition,
Also,

9 Tell your students to write their summary, using the points you have agreed on, some of the formulae (beginnings/endings/connectors) and remembering the word limit. It should come out something like this:

'According to the writer there are five symptoms of old age. Firstly, you grow deaf and can't hear the phone ringing. Secondly, you fall easily, which makes travel impossible and leads to a change in behaviour. In addition, your body begins to demand constant attention, giving an overwhelming medical schedule. You also become absent-minded and misplace things. Lastly, you forget things and so can't remember names and faces. In general, you become dependent on others.'

This summary has seventy-five words.

10 Remind the class of the steps you went through to produce this summary and write them on the board:

- Identify what is at the core of the summary question
- Find the core items (in this case the symptoms)
- Add what else the summary requires (in this case the consequences)
- Connect and order
- Write the summary

Stress to your students that this method of summary writing, unlike many traditional methods involves not reducing the original text but finding the core of the new text and expanding around it.

VARIATIONS

1 If you wish to approach this text not only for summary writing but to work on the other types of questions found in the Proficiency Examination, a possible set of questions is provided in the Worksheet on page 104, which helps both in this and in a more general comprehension of the text. Make copies and distribute one each to the class.

ANSWERS TO WORKSHEET FOR ACTIVITY 4.4

1 'But old age is not all suffering' (line 46) marks the beginning of the second section. The first part is about the bad things of old age, the second about the good ones.

2 stage, age, dimension – accept any appropriate answer (*janma* actually means 'birth').

3 That he's going deaf.

4 Someone who is mischievous or plays tricks, a goblin. (The reference is, of course, to the character in Shakespeare's *The Tempest*.)

5 Gravity has no mercy, no one escapes its power.

6 Changing/Improving my behaviour.

7 That the elderly have a natural way of falling asleep, which they often use.

8 Old age can lead to regret that youth is past, 'good old days' seem distant, contemporaries die, leaving the elderly person increasingly lonely.

9 There are many examples of humour. Here are just a few:

a being 'blissfully unaware of the [telephone] ringing' (line 6) – a paradox since normally it would be a problem not to hear the telephone

b 'A Caliban seems to be at your elbow' (line 13) – the personification of an annoyance

c 'Your medical schedule becomes overwhelming' (line 27) – ironical exaggeration

d deliberately playing with the meaning of a fixed expression, in this instance the title 'Decline and Fall' (line 30)

e the imagery of such phrases as 'more mental space is usurped by memory' (line 67)

10 The writer has to adjust to a different way of living as he gets older.

2 Above we summarised only part of the text, as required by the task. This is typical of summary tasks in Proficiency Examinations and typical of real life – we normally select information from a text rather than summarise it all. Some of my students, accustomed to summary more as an academic exercise, often ask me how to summarise the whole text. The process is essentially the same, expansion from the core, except that we first have to identify the core, that is to say what the text is centrally about. Invite suggestions from your students. Come to an agreement with them and proceed as above (summarised in Step 10), bearing in mind the different core. A suitable core would be 'The disadvantages and advantages of old age'.

NOTE

One could criticise Narayan's text for the mixed use of *one* and *you*, and for other minor points. You may wish to draw your students' attention to them. However, personally, I find them trivial in what for me is a very rich and serene piece of writing.

ACKNOWLEDGEMENT

I first described summarising through mind maps, as a technique for learners of a foreign language, in 'Notes, summaries and compositions' (Cranmer 1985).

TEXT FOR ACTIVITY 4.4

It is immaterial what the 'plus' signifies or how far it goes. One changes radically at 80 – until you reach the 364th day past 79 you are Mr So-and-So, but on the 365th day you enter a new janma. Old age sets in with the precision of a planet in orbit and the insidious moving belt takes you down a gentle slope
5 unnoticed until you see others at home proceeding towards the telephone while you are blissfully unaware of the ringing.

Let a fellow octogenarian correct me if I generalise that the left ear drum is the first to be switched off. You don't notice until you find that others around mumble a great deal and utter unclear sentences. Faculties are switched off
10 one by one, beginning at the top.

Absent-mindedness is the first symptom. Your hands act independently, just misplacing and hiding papers, documents and keys so that your waking hours are spent searching for something or other. A Caliban seems to be at your elbow, plaguing you, enjoying the torments he inflicts.
15 Next, you forget names and faces. Familiar face but who is he? Or the name is all right, we were classmates of course, but I can't remember what he looks like. We even had photographs, but they are lost. General forgetfulness starts thus, a blessing. Forgetfulness is a boon to be cherished; remembrance could be a torture sometimes.
20 Travelling downward from the top, senility starts. The apparatus called the human body begins to demand constant attention, while hermits advise: 'Learn to forget your body. Ignore it and you will attain divine peace.' Impossible at this stage. Every moment one corner of the system or another clamours for attention major or minor – maybe a scratch or an ache or some-
25 thing serious. Whatever it may be, it rings an alarm bell. Ultimately a dozen different specialists have to monitor your system from time to time to reassure you that you will continue to be alive, with dos and don'ts. Your medical schedule becomes overwhelming.

When I think of Gibbon, I admire his genius in naming his Roman history
30 *Decline and Fall* for they are a natural sequence. It applies to Eighty Plus: with decline one has to dread a fall too, which seems built-in. My doctor always cautions, 'Don't fall'. I respect his advice, no doubt, but gravity is ruthless.

Tumbling down is inevitable in old age. I have suffered two falls in three years. On both occasions I realised how totally helpless one feels – when you
35 start falling, no power on earth can arrest your fall.

The pull of gravity is inexorable; if it could also tunnel through the core of the earth, it would perhaps not rest till you found yourself at the Antipodes. Luckily I was not broken or maimed, I got off with shock and bruises. Now I give due respect to Nature's authority by mending my conduct: never rise
40 abruptly from my seat or the bed, never venture to walk without a four-pronged 'walker' in hand and also a human support to clutch – a precaution for survival.

Cranmer *Motivating High Level Learners*
© Addison Wesley Longman Limited 1996 Photocopiable *(continued)*

Past 80, one becomes dependent on so many helping hands. Travel becomes impossible, unthinkable. Every little movement assumes the dimensions of a manoeuvre – to be deeply thought out and managed.

But old age is not all suffering. There are certain benefits too. For one thing, you find everyone considerate in a hundred ways. Age brings on certain unasked privileges. People avoid hurting your feelings and are ever cautious and considerate and treat you as if old age were an achievement.

Your own interests change. First and foremost, women look worshipful rather than sensual. Next you realise the unimportance of possessions, acquisitions, and enjoy the pleasure of dispossessing yourself of everything and watching others enjoy life.

Fewer irritations in life are felt because of your defective hearing. You don't fret any more at the idiocies on TV. You can always operate the God-given shutters, one's eyelids, which – properly used – can shut off any spectacle. So, also, if you don't wish to hear, the simplest method is to plug your ears with the little fingers in hand, which seem to be made to measure. Thus you have natural facilities to see no evil, hear no evil and speak no evil, if you resist the temptation to discuss the newspaper headlines with others. At Eighty Plus, you learn to attain peace of mind by these measures. It takes time and practice to understand your potentialities and exert your inner strength. You must reach a minimum of 80 years to mellow and realise your potentialities.

Memory is one factor that must be curbed rigorously. Memory and hope are two elements that are inborn. Hope is potent in earlier life, its area diminishes unnoticed in later life, and more mental space is usurped by memory, which is pleasant up to a stage. I say up to a stage, which is to be determined by the nature of one's experience.

Music when soft voices die,
Vibrates in the memory –

So said Shelley. It may not always be 'music'. For most of us, recollection is painful – a past moment or a face brings on an overwhelming mood of sadness. To forget the past and live in the present, relishing the quality of every moment as it comes and letting it also pass without regret, realising the inevitability of the Eternal flux, is the practical way to exist in peace.

© R. K. Narayan

WORKSHEET FOR ACTIVITY 4.4

Read the text and answer these questions.

1 This essay falls naturally into two distinct sections. What marks the division between these two sections?

....

....

2 You won't find the word *janma* (line 3) in an English dictionary. From the context, what do you suppose it means?

....

....

3 What point is the writer trying to make when he mentions 'others at home proceeding towards the telephone while you are blissfully unaware of the ringing' (line 5)?

....

4 Judging from the context, what do you suppose a 'Caliban' is (line 13)?

....

5 Why does the writer describe gravity as 'ruthless' (line 32)?

....

6 Explain what the writer means by 'mending my conduct' (line 39).

....

7 What point is the writer making when he describes eyelids as 'God-given shutters' (line 55)?

....

8 Why do you think that the writer says 'For most of us, recollection is painful' (line 72)?

....

....

9 The writer creates humour in a variety of ways. Find three passages you find humorous. How does the writer create his humorous effect in each case?

....

....

....

10 The writer entitled this essay 'Old age, new life'. Explain why this title is appropriate.

....

....

....

THE RANDOM OBJECT

FOCUS
What to do when ideas won't come

MATERIALS
OHP and transparency (optional)

TIME
50–90 minutes

This activity assumes you have already done Activities 4.2 *The brainstorm plan* and/or 4.3 *The mind map plan*. To avoid possible confusion, I do this activity at least a month before or after the ten creative principles (see Activities 3.8 *'Pigs might fly'* and 3.9 *Creative principles applied*), with which this activity has a good deal in common.

Preparation

If available, prepare an OHP transparency as indicated in Steps 3 and 4 below. Otherwise, you will need to use the board. Choose a really dull composition title. I shall take 'My first day at school'.

Procedure

1 Pose the problem of what to do if you are trying to do a brainstorm or mind map plan but ideas won't come. If you have already worked on the ten creative principles, then running through these may well generate ideas that can be added to the plan. However, not all titles respond well to this kind of approach. Explain to your students that you are going to show them a(nother) way of generating ideas.

2 Give your class the title and ask them to write down ideas for a composition in the form of a brainstorm or mind map plan. If they groan at the title, as my students usually do, remind them that the whole point of this activity is to show them how to generate ideas when they lack inspiration, so you have to demonstrate the technique with an uninspired title.

3 Ask them to think of an object – the first thing that comes into their head. Get them to write it down on a separate sheet of paper at the top of the page. When they have done that, ask them to choose another completely different object and write that halfway down the same page. Tell them that you want them to write down the characteristics of their objects. Put examples such as these on an OHP or write them on the board:

gramophone record
● round
● has grooves
● goes round and round
● it gets scratched and crackles
● sometimes gets stuck in a groove
● costs money
● becoming obsolete because of compact discs
● plays music and words

cup of tea
- something to drink
- refreshing
- hot or cold or lukewarm
- with or without milk
- with or without sugar
- strong or weak
- leaves or tea bags
- do I like it?

Now tell them to list characteristics in the same way for their own objects.

4 When they have completed their lists, tell them that they are going to relate the objects and their characteristics to the composition title to generate further ideas. Exemplify this by linking the objects and their characteristics above to the title you are working on, in this instance 'My first day at school'. Start with the gramophone record:

- round: you could write about the shape (design) of the school
- has grooves: what the school consisted of
- goes round and round: the movement of people in the school
- gets scratched or crackles: the condition of the school
- sometimes gets stuck in a groove: teachers who were boring and repeated themselves
- costs money: cost of school books, other equipment
- becoming obsolete because of compact discs: was it a new school or rather out of date?
- plays music or words: what subjects were there? music?

This has already generated a lot of ideas, but the cup of tea will add a good many more:

- something to drink: the facilities for lunch, snacks, etc.
- refreshing: were some lessons more refreshing than others?
- hot or cold or lukewarm: was it hot, cold or lukewarm in the school? were the teachers and pupils hot, cold or lukewarm?
- with or without milk: were there any choices?
- with or without sugar: was there any 'sugar' to make the day sweeter?
- strong or weak: was the discipline strong or weak?
- leaves or tea bags: (I couldn't find a way to relate this to the topic!)
- do I like it?: was the first day enjoyable?

Tell your students to do the same with the characteristics of their objects, adding the ideas thus generated to the ideas they originally wrote in Steps 2 and 3. Allow fifteen to twenty minutes to do this.

5 When everyone is ready, ask them how many ideas they now have. They will probably have so many that they won't know what to do with them all. Now they must add these ideas to their

original plan. Bearing in mind the length of composition they have to write, ask them to select from all the ideas in their plan the ones they want to use. The best way to do this is to put a single line through the ideas they intend to omit. (In this way they can still read what they originally wrote, in case they change their minds.) Then ask them to proceed with ordering their plan in the usual way.

6 Tell them to write a composition. You can use the title you have been working on, but I prefer to set a new title so that they have to go through this whole procedure again by themselves.

NOTE
This technique is just as valuable when preparing an oral presentation.

ACKNOWLEDGEMENTS
The use of random objects in this way is based on Edward de Bono's random word principle, which I first read about in *Teaching Thinking* (de Bono 1976). I first wrote about this use in 'Teaching more advanced learners' (Cranmer 1990/91).

LETHARGY AND THE LEMON

This activity illustrates another use of the random object principle, this time applied to a problem arising with a class. It provides a framework for examining the problem and considering possible solutions. If you have already done Activity 4.5 *The random object* with your students, they will be familiar with the random object procedure and you will be able to deal directly with the problem. If not, you will need to talk them through this procedure as well as tackling the problem. This activity is not appropriate unless both teacher and class are willing to confront such internal problems and seek solutions.

4.6

FOCUS
Solving the problems that arise with a class

MATERIALS
None

TIME
20 minutes +

Procedure

1 Make the problem you want to solve known to the class and write it at the top of the board in the middle. (An example of one I once had to tackle is given below.) The problem may be one that you have identified or one that your students have drawn to your attention. Ask them to think of a physical object at random and call it out. Write the first object called out in the middle of the board.

2 Ask your students to work in pairs and write down the characteristics of the object. Allow five minutes for this and then ask for feedback. Write their answers on the board around the object.

3 Ask the class how these characteristics might relate to the problem at the top of the board. Give an example and write it beside

the characteristic concerned. Then ask them to work in pairs and try to do the same with the other characteristics. Allow up to ten minutes for this and then ask for feedback. Write their points on the board beside the characteristic involved.

4 Use the points that have been made as a basis for discussion of the problem. Try to come to some kind of conclusion as to how to deal with it and what concrete steps that you or they will take to see that it doesn't recur.

An example of a problem I had to solve:

With one class I had a mid-year crisis. For a term we had worked very well together but in the middle of the second term they all became terribly lethargic, attendance dropped, homework didn't get done, some students began to arrive habitually late. I put this problem to them one lesson.

I began by pointing out that I felt it was very positive that we could discuss this problem at all, as this indicated there was plenty of goodwill in the class, something essential if we were to resolve the problem. On this occasion the object was one that I chose: a lemon. Below are the characteristics I identified and how I felt they might relate to our problem. We discussed the points for half an hour or so. Although we did not come up with clear suggestions for the future, the fact that we had discussed the whole problem thoroughly was enough to result in a rapid improvement.

Lemons are:
- yellow: could the course be more colourful, i.e. interesting?
- sour: is there anything distasteful in the course?
- refreshing: do we need to look at ways to make the course more refreshing, e.g. with more variety, or one-off lessons to make a change?
- vitamins: the nutrients of the course – ought we to include more grammar exercises, vocabulary activities?
- acid: should I be more acid and not quite so 'sweet' with them?
- shape: how aware are the students of the shape of the course as I see it?
- harvested in winter: there is a need for times of growth and times of harvest. The growth may not be visible till the fruit is ripe.
- I like them: everyone has their own tastes.
- cool: should I be more hot-tempered about lateness, lack of homework, etc.? (There was a general feeling that I should!)
- smooth with bumps: life (and courses) are not always smooth.
- hard skin, soft inside: are we concentrating too much on superficial problems and not getting to the heart of the matter?

A discussion of this last point led to an important conclusion. It seemed that the problems we were feeling were probably not so much a matter of what we had identified: not enough homework, not enough grammar, not being made to read enough outside, not working hard enough, not being challenged enough, bad time of year, poor attendance – the immediate symptoms we were seeing. Rather, we were coming up against a series of new realities: learning at more advanced levels is not a series of easily identifiable steps (as is a grammar-based syllabus, for example), that the available books at this level often leave a lot to be desired, that expectations needed to be altered, that there was a major problem of lack of commitment especially in terms of time spent on learning English outside class, that there were strong emotional blocks against making the necessary commitment, that it was hard always to see the relevance of what they were doing.

Almost two years after this lesson I happened to have lunch with a former student from the class. He said to me, 'I often think about you and the classes we had, but the one that made the deepest impression on me was the one about the lemon.'

PLUS, MINUS AND INTERESTING

Teachers, educational psychologists and specialists in applied linguistics are not alone in having insights into the issues involved in learning and teaching foreign languages. Our students notice things to which we may be blind. We may also want to share our own concerns about issues of relevance to our teaching situation. The PMI (Plus, Minus and Interesting), developed by Edward de Bono, provides a framework for discussing these issues.

Procedure

1 Choose an issue relevant to your teaching situation. It may be one that you feel is important or one raised by your students. Turn the issue into an extreme and thus provocative statement, or take something so obviously desirable that it is not normally discussed. Here are some examples:

Exams and tests should be abolished.
Only English should be spoken in class.
All education should be free of charge.
A substantial piece of homework should be set every lesson.
Schools should be abolished.
Fees should be retained at their present level next year.

Notice that all of these statements include *should* and several statements are made stronger by including *only*, *all* and *every*. Write the statement you are going to work on at the top of the board.

2 Draw up three columns on the board. Head them P, M and I, respectively. Ask the class to guess what they stand for. (It is most unlikely they will succeed, so you will need to tell them. Making them guess, however, does draw their attention to the letters and

4.7

FOCUS
A framework for discussing and sharing insights into learning and teaching issues

MATERIALS
None

TIME
50–90 minutes

thus helps to fix the framework in their minds.) Tell them to copy what is on the board into their notebooks.

3 Put the class into groups of three or four. Ask them to discuss the statement and draw up lists of plus, minus and interesting points about it. Appoint a secretary in each group to do this. Emphasise that you are just interested in ideas, no matter how absurd or fantastic – this is not an exercise in reality! Allow at least twenty minutes for this step.

4 Put the students back in full class formation and ask the secretaries to tell you the plus points their group made. Write the points on the board and tell the class to copy them into their notebooks. Do the same for the minus points and finally the interesting points. As different groups often have similar points it is worth asking around to see which group has expressed the point best. Discussion often arises spontaneously in this phase. Encourage this unless you are in danger of running out of time. Here is an example of the points raised when I looked at the statement 'Exams and tests should be abolished' with one class:

Plus	Minus	Interesting
Students would not suffer from nerves	Students wouldn't learn the facts	You could use continuous evaluation
It would leave more time for teaching	Some students work better under test pressure	Students could write their own tests or test each other
It would be fairer on those who don't have an exam temperament	You would lose a good way of co-ordinating the marking of work in different classes at the same level	No one would cheat
It would be fairer on those who have an off-day or for whom the questions aren't suitable		

5 Discuss with the class what morals might be drawn from the points in relation to the reality of the learning/teaching situation you are working in and what action you might feel appropriate. The 'Interesting' points are often particularly useful.

COMMENT

Apparently uncontroversial statements and absurd points often contain the seeds of very important issues. For example, the statement 'Only English should be spoken in class' may for many teachers and students seem self-evident, yet putting it into a PMI framework provides a way into discussion of why this may be very difficult to achieve (arising above all from the M column).

ACKNOWLEDGEMENT
I first learnt about the PMI from *Teaching Thinking* (De Bono 1976).

THE PMI COMPOSITION

4.8

FOCUS
Applying the plus, minus, interesting technique to composition writing

MATERIALS
None

TIME
50–90 minutes

Students at university or preparing for Cambridge examinations (FCE and especially CPE), for example, often need to write discursive essays. These may require them to discuss both sides of an argument ('advantages and disadvantages', 'for and against', a balanced essay simply with the instruction 'Discuss'), or just one side of it (usually their own opinion), or a combination of both. To write a good, full-length essay (i.e. three hundred or more words), irrespective of the task, it is always important to consider all sides of the issue in question. The PMI (see Activity 4.7) provides an excellent framework for doing this. Although the PMI looks like a plan for a balanced essay, it is importantly different:

a it is a thinking tool and may therefore include the unreal, the impossible and the illogical – for playing around with. An essay plan is very real and must be down-to-earth, possible and logical

b the PMI has an 'Interesting' column, which falls outside the parameters of the classic 'for and against'/'advantages and disadvantages' framework

In this activity students learn how to use the PMI as a thinking tool to generate ideas and then convert it into an essay plan. To go through this process is slow and time-consuming, but with regular practice students learn to do it very quickly. If your students are already used to the PMI framework (e.g. in Activity 4.7), it will help here, but it is by no means essential.

Procedure

1 Write the title of the essay your students are going to write at the top of the board in the centre. If it is already provocative it can remain as it stands. Here are two examples of titles that are already sufficiently provocative:

Aid should not be given to developing countries.
Prisons should be abolished.

If the title is less provocative, ask your students to make it more provocative. Remember that for the time being you are merely thinking around an issue, not answering a question. Here are examples of statements/questions that have been made more provocative:

People should eat less meat.

– changed to a more extreme position:

Everyone should be vegetarian.

The population explosion needs to be controlled.

– changed to a more specific statement:

Couples must only have one child.

Is euthanasia morally justifiable?

– changed to an affirmation:

Euthanasia is morally justifiable.

Write the more provocative version beneath the title.

2 Draw up three columns on the board. Head them P, M and I respectively. If this is the first time your students have done a PMI, ask them to guess what the letters stand for (see Activity 4.7 Step 2). Tell them to write down the title (plus the more provocative version) and the PMI framework.

3 Put the class into pairs and ask them to discuss and write down in note form the plus, minus and interesting points about the statement. If we take the statement 'Everyone should be vegetarian', we might get the following points:

Plus	Minus	Interesting
healthier	difficult to get enough protein for hard physical work	in some parts of the world, e.g. parts of India, everyone is vegetarian
cheaper		
reduces aggression in people	would reduce variety in cooking	
would provide more work in agriculture for people tending crops	people in meat industry would be out of a job	vogue in current Western culture
	what would we do with surplus livestock?	
	limits personal freedom	

4 If you altered the original title to make it more provocative, return to the original now. From the PMI ideas cut any that are not relevant, which is rarely the case, and make any necessary adaptations to make other points relevant. Taking the vegetarian issue, the only point that might be cut is 'would reduce variety in cooking', since if a less radical stance were taken and some meat allowed, this would no longer be true. Some of the other points need minor adaptation but most remain equally relevant as they stand.

5 Tell your students to look at the Plus and Minus points and try to identify any that are parallel (the same or the converse). For example, the Plus point that it would provide more work tending crops is paralleled by the point that people in the meat industry would be out of a job (a converse relationship).

Get them to draw a line between parallel points. For any points that have no parallel, tell your students to try to think of one. This is nearly always possible and generates a lot of further ideas. When they have done this, tell them once again to draw a line between the parallel points. This is the end of the idea-generation phase.

6 Now begin the organising phase. This will depend on the task. If the essay is of the balanced type, continue with this Step 6; if it is just giving one side of the argument, go on to Step 7 instead.

In a balanced essay, the next step is to decide upon the order you are going to present your points. Ask your students to go through the points (parallel pairs of points in most instances) and decide the order they want to present these in their essay, numbering them accordingly. If it is relevant to the task, the Interesting points often form the basis for a good final paragraph – these need ordering too.

If you feel your students need it, this is the point where you can teach/revise appropriate connectors. Three kinds are particularly relevant here:

List connectors
Firstly/Secondly/Thirdly . . . Lastly/Finally
In the first/second/third place . . .

Connectors of addition
and
also
In addition,
Not only that but . . .
Furthermore,

Connectors of contrast
but
On the one hand, . . . On the other, . . .
While/Whilst

Go on to Step 8.

7 Explain to your students that with a one-sided essay the next stage is to decide which side of the argument they are going to support and whether the interesting points are relevant to their argument. Tell them to do so. Then they need to decide on the order they want to present their points, including the interesting ones if relevant. Ask them to number the points they intend to make. Tell them that to be convincing they will also need to counter the arguments against them. In doing so they will need to use connectors of concession. If necessary, teach/revise the following connectors and the constructions that go with them. By way of example, we will concede that 'Fish is healthier to eat than meat' (argument against), while affirming that 'Many people prefer meat' (Your argument).

With the adverbials *However, Nevertheless, Nonetheless,* and *Even so,*:

concession	affirmation
(argument against you)	*(your argument)*
Fish is healthier than meat.	*However,* many people prefer meat.
	Nevertheless, many . . .
	Nonetheless, many . . .
	Even so, many . . .

With the prepositions *In spite of* and *Despite*:

concession	affirmation
(argument against you)	*(your argument)*
In spite of fish being healthier to eat than meat,	
Despite fish . . .	many people prefer meat.

With the conjunctions *Although* and *Even though*:

concession	affirmation
(argument against you)	*(your argument)*
Although fish is healthier to eat than meat	
Even though fish . . .	many people prefer meat.

If necessary, also teach/revise list connectors and connectors of addition, as given in Step 6, above.

8 Tell your students to write an opening 'topic' sentence for the essay – one that determines what the essay will be about. They may need to develop this further to clarify the parameters of the essay, e.g. by stating which side of the argument they intend to take in a one-sided essay. Remind them about paragraphing – each of their points should be developed into a short paragraph. Also remind them of the importance of a good final paragraph, e.g. a strong final point or referring back in some way to the opening paragraph, to give a sense of conclusion. They are now ready to start writing.

ACKNOWLEDGEMENT
I first learnt about the PMI as a thinking tool from *Teaching Thinking* (De Bono 1976).

CHAPTER 5

Feedback

'The child is father of the man.'
  William Wordsworth

All the activities in Chapters 1 to 4 are in preparation for some kind of output, usually in writing. This chapter focuses on various aspects of feedback: correction of written work, following it up in readiness for the next piece, advising students in the light of feedback and going about formal assessment.

AFTER CORRECTION I

Beyond reminding students to check and edit, and getting them used to allocating time to do both when writing a composition, there is little you can do to encourage these good habits in the short term. In the long term, however, you can train students to be more aware of what to check for in their own work by going to a good deal of trouble in correcting and following up corrections. This activity and the following one describe the procedure my various classes and I have adopted after a lot of discussion and many attempts at different correction techniques and ways of following up. They have become one of the most central elements in most of the courses I teach from a mid-intermediate level upwards, providing a regular source of class and individual language feedback and helping students to feel they are getting plenty of solid language work as well as the rather different activities described in this book.

Preparation

Correct all that is incorrect in your students' written work. I find that this is what my students expect of me and it provides fully honest feedback on their work. I also like to tick any specially good turns of phrase and comment positively on what I think they have done well. To avoid masses of red ink I normally use green ink, which I find equally clear and much less punitive. To go through a composition painstakingly is a slow business, but if students write compositions conscientiously, they have every right to expect the same conscientiousness of us, and followed up properly, it is time well spent. Do not write a grade or mark on the composition, but keep a record of it.

5.1

FOCUS
Making sure learners benefit from correction; Encouraging checking and editing

MATERIALS
None

TIME
50 minutes +

Procedure

1 Return the compositions to their writers. Ask your students to go through their compositions numbering the corrections you have made from one to however many there are. Point out that if you have corrected spelling or punctuation, they must include these like any other correction.

2 Meanwhile, write these four categories on the board:

a silly mistakes
b translation problems
c other problems – you understand the correction
d other problems – you don't understand the correction

Ask your students to copy this down. Then tell them to decide which category each of your corrections falls into and to write the number of each correction beside the appropriate category heading. Thus corrections 2, 3, 6, 9, 12, 14, 22, 27 and 29 might be category **a** (silly mistakes), while 1, 4, 5, 11, 13, 16, 17, 18 and 24 might be category **b** (translation problems), etc.

3 Explain the division into 'mistakes' – what your students know in principle but got wrong – and 'problems' – what they got wrong because they don't know how to express it. Remind them that everyone makes silly mistakes, but they should try to keep them to a minimum. If there are more than two or three (and there usually are), either they are not checking their work properly or simply not paying sufficient attention to accuracy, and this needs putting right. Tell them you are going to work with them on the problems, i.e. what they still need to work on.

4 a If you are working with a monolingual class there may be quite a lot of translation problems that have arisen in several compositions. In any case, many others in the class could easily have come to grief if they had been trying to express the same idea. So go round the class asking each student what translation problems they had. Most of such problems tend to involve the use of a construction from the students' own language which doesn't exist in English. Write the errors and corrections on the board for everyone to learn from, explaining as necessary. If you have a multilingual class, it is unfortunately difficult to implement this very valuable step. Dealing with a set of translation problems tends to take me an hour or more except with very advanced classes, but my students often comment on how valuable they find this.

b If you don't deal with the translation problems, treat the category **c** problems in the same way as in Step 4a, so that others can learn from them too. If I deal with the translation problems, I leave out this stage, as it all gets too much.

5 Deal with the category **d** problems – these have to be dealt with as the students do not understand why you have corrected them.

Some of these problems may be very individual, in which case I usually speak to the student concerned at the end of the class, but generally these problems are also of relevance to others in the class so I put up the error and correction on the board, see if anyone else in the class can explain the correction and, if not, I explain it myself.

6 Ask your students to go through their compositions and underline any words or phrases they are especially glad they got right. Nearly always they have made guesses or taken risks and got them right. This is one way of making them feel good about this. I sometimes get them to give themselves a round of applause at this point.

7 Divide the class into groups of three or four. Ask them to look at one another's compositions to decide which they feel is best in their group and why. For one of several reasons, they often come to no conclusion:

a diplomacy prevents them from singling out one composition
b genuinely, none is noticeably better than the others
c each composition has merits in different areas – encourage discussion of this

The conclusion is less important than discussion of the merits. Monitor the groups and join in if you feel this would help. When they have come to a conclusion as to which (if any) is best, tell them if you agree or not. Ask them to write down a list of the good points they have seen in the various compositions. Give out the marks, either while they are together if you don't feel this will cause embarrassment, or more discreetly by speaking to individuals or handing them a slip of paper with the mark on.

5.2

FOCUS
Making sure
learners benefit
from correction;
Encouraging
checking and
editing

MATERIALS
Loose-leaf file

TIME
50 minutes +

AFTER CORRECTION II

This is the way I go through corrections on the second and subsequent occasions.

Preparation

Ask your students to get a loose-leaf file, their 'follow-up book', and bring it to class whenever you are going over a set of written work. Correct the written work.

Procedure

1 The first time you do this, ask your students to divide their 'follow-up book' up into sections: silly mistakes, translation problems, other problems, things I got right, good things to put in written work, spelling corrections.
2 Follow the procedure as in Activity 5.1, but summarise Steps 1 and 2 and cut Step 3, as this explanation is no longer necessary. Get your students to enter the various points – the positive points as well as the things that need further work – in their follow-up book. They need to note:

- silly mistakes
- translation problems (this is best in the form of a mini bilingual dictionary, so that they can readily see how the problem has arisen)
- other problems (this forms only one category, since after you have explained anything they are unclear about, there are no longer corrections they don't understand)
- things they got right (what you ticked while correcting and anything else they are specially pleased they got right)
- good things to put in written work

At home they write out the spelling corrections five times each.
3 From time to time, ask to see their follow-up books, to check that they have done spelling corrections. (I always warn them beforehand if I intend to do this.) On the same occasion get them to look back at what they have written, above all to see if any problems or silly mistakes recur. A silly mistake that recurs is not a silly mistake but a problem that needs to be tackled. If other problems recur, the student concerned needs to consider why and what she or he intends to do about it.

NOTES

a I asked a class if they could think of a better way of dealing with spelling than writing out the correct form five times. The only suggestion was writing it out ten times.
b When students have been working with me for a while and are used to my marking system, I often ask them to give themselves a mark. I either confirm this or suggest what I think is appropriate.

This approach has many advantages. With all this feedback, they begin to get a very clear picture of where they stand – what's going right and what isn't – and, I find, begin to assess themselves quite realistically. When their assessment and mine differ, we can discuss the differences and see why, usually, I would give a higher mark than they would.

COUNSELLING

I find, particularly after tests or at the end of a course, that students often feel the need to discuss their results and more general progress with their teacher. Unless you have some system for answering this need out of class, you need to allocate class time for this at regular intervals.

If you are with the same students for more than a short course, it is important to counsel them for the first time early enough for remedial action to be possible. In an annual course beginning in October, I would expect the first session to be in early December. I consistently find that sympathetic but frank counselling leads to a strong feeling of solidarity between student and teacher.

Preparation

Choose a suitable task for the class to be getting on with while you are talking to individual members.

Procedure

1 Explain to the class that you would like to talk to each member of the class about their test results/progress. Set the task you prepared for the rest of the class.
2 Talk to each student in turn about their work. You may be able to do this by going round the class to each student, you may want to ask them to come to your desk or to a space outside the classroom – use your discretion to choose a suitable place where you will not be overheard. I find it is important first to ascertain the students' perspective on their work and then to confirm, contest or comment on what they say. They and you may have little to say if all is running smoothly, in which case you can move rapidly on to the next student. With others you may need to talk at length about difficulties and possible solutions.

NOTE

In some discussions personal problems come out, some students may break down in tears over a poor result, hence the importance of privacy in these interviews.

5.3

FOCUS
Discussing progress with students

MATERIALS
None

TIME
5 minutes per student

ACKNOWLEDGEMENT
Counselling, having been a practice among a few teachers of examination classes at the British Council, Lisbon, has more recently
become part of the general system with all classes. I am unsure
how far I may have learnt the idea from others or was myself an
instigator.

5.4

FOCUS
Leading students
to be realistic
about their final
grade

MATERIALS
A copy of the
Self-assessment
sheet (adapted to
your own
circumstances)
for each student

TIME
30 minutes

FORMAL ASSESSMENT

There are many ways in which formal assessment runs rather contrary to the philosophy of this book. The reality is, however, that
many of us are in teaching contexts where we are required to make
formal assessments of our students. This activity shows a way of
going about this in a spirit of openness.

Preparation

Prepare a Self-assessment sheet. The one on page 122 is appropriate
for my current teaching context: my students are not allowed to
miss any of their four tests, they have to do homework, they have to
attend at least two-thirds of the lessons and are expected to participate actively in English; their tests count for 60% of their final grade,
the rest, including my discretion, counts for 40%. Adapt the sheet to
include the points you would need to take into account in your own
context. The 'General' section is crucial.

Procedure

1 Give each student a copy of the Self-assessment sheet.
2 Talk them through the sheet, explaining anything you feel needs
   clarification, and then ask them to complete it. Assure them that
   you regard this activity as important and will take what they write
   into account when awarding their final grades. Help them with
   any factual information, for example, about their marks or the
   number of absences they have had.
3 When they have finished, collect the sheets in.

AFTERWARDS
When you come to awarding the final grades, look through the information your students have given you. Look at the grade they feel is
right for them and the justification they give. If you agree that this
grade gives a fair reflection of their performance, give it. If not,
adjust it to what you consider fair, but taking into account what they
have written.

NOTE

This point-by-point procedure, taking all possible elements for assessment into account, by and large leads to a realistic self-assessment on the part of the students. The grades they have received during the course speak for themselves and they realise that their final grade must reflect these. The first time I tried this out, of about seventy students, spread over three classes, I agreed with the marks of about sixty, only two awarded themselves one mark out of twenty more than I felt was justified and the remainder gave themselves one too few.

'Like the meeting of the seagulls and the waves we meet and come near.
The seagulls fly off, the waves roll away and we depart.'
   Rabrindinath Tagore

SELF-ASSESSMENT SHEET

Tests

Of the four tests, how many did you do? ....

What grade did you get in each?   Test 1 ....

        Test 2 ....

        Test 3 ....

        Test 4 ....

What was your average mark? ....

Homework

Have you done your homework regularly? ....

What about the compositions?
Have you done them regularly/sometimes/rarely? ....

What about the grammar exercises?
Have you done them regularly/sometimes/rarely? ....

Did you do a project? ....

What grade did you receive? ....

Speaking

Would you say you speak English better than you write? ....

Less well? ....

About the same? ....

Do you speak English in class or
do you tend to lapse into your own language? ....

How do you respond to reminders to speak in English? ....

Attendance

Have you been to

    virtually all lessons? ....

    at least three-quarters of the lessons? ....

    the minimum number of lessons you have to attend? ....

    fewer than two-thirds of the lessons? ....

Have you been consistently punctual or
do you tend to arrive late? ....

General

In the light of all your answers above, what grade
[specify the scale] do you realistically expect to be
awarded? ....

Justify this grade.

....

....

Bibliography

Berger, J 1972 *Ways of Seeing* BBC Publications

Buzan, T 1974, rev. 1982, 1989 *Use Your Head* BBC Publications

Cranmer, D 1985 Notes, summaries and compositions. In Matthews, A et al. (ed.) *At the Chalkface* Edward Arnold (1985)

Cranmer, D 1990/91 Teaching more advanced learners. *British Council Newsletter for Portuguese Teachers of English* **XI**, 1, 2 and 3 (pp. 21–5, 21–9, 28–30)

Cranmer, D and Laroy, C 1992 *Musical Openings* Longman

Davis, P and Rinvolucri, M 1990 *The Confidence Book* Longman

De Bono, E 1976 *Teaching Thinking* Penguin

Fritzen, S J 1987 *Relações Humanas Interpessoais* Vozes (Petrópolis)

Kiefer-Dicks, D 1993 Exploring the black hole with your Swiss students. *English Teachers' Association Switzerland (ETAS) Newsletter Lausanne Branch* **11** (1)

Lindstromberg, S (ed.) 1990 *The Recipe Book* Longman

Lindstromberg, S (ed.) (forthcoming) *The Standby Book* CUP

Morgan, J and Rinvolucri, M 1983 *Once Upon a Time* CUP

Munari, B 1987 *Fantasia* Editorial Presença (Lisbon); originally published by Giuseppe Laterza & Figli (Bari)

Puchta, H and Schratz, M 1993 *Teaching Teenagers* Longman

Ristad, E 1982 *A Soprano on Her Head* Real People Press

Sion, C (ed.) 1991 *More Recipes For Tired Teachers* Addison-Wesley

Tagore, R 1917 *Stray Birds* Macmillan